Twenty Years in Retail
What Happens Behind the Scenes
Cassie Laurell

Twenty Years in Retail: What Happens Behind the Scenes

Copyright © 2025 by Cassie Laurell

Published by Cassie Laurell

ISBN 979-8-218-71584-7

First Paperback Edition: June 2025

Printed in the United States of America

This book is a memoir, based on true events. Some inaccuracies may be caused by my recollection of past events. Some names and identifying details have been changed to protect the privacy of the individuals involved. Dialogue is not a literal transcription of words spoken.

Contents

1

It All Started at Linens 'n Things

In September 2005, like millions of Americans in need, I started working in a retail store. Retail is a labor sector that typically engulfs people strapped for money, such as individuals with low resources trying to make a living, students trying to pay tuition or college loans, retirees trying to supplement their income, employees seeking a second occupation to increase the number of their working hours, and single mothers struggling to pay their bills. The common denominator of retail workers is usually the impossibility to find a better paying job, due to lack of skills or experience. I belonged to the category of divorced mothers with insufficient income. Although I had past teaching experience, after following my husband to Europe and living there for ten years, it was impossible for me to go back to academia. I had no recent publications and I had two children who required time and attention. After multiple failed attempts to get hired in a variety of professional work settings, I contacted a staffing agency. The agency examined my resume and told me that I was "not marketable" because of my age and because I lacked the experience necessary to be placed in any job. I was about 50 years old, I had college degrees, but I couldn't be placed in any kind of employment.

That staffing agency opened my eyes. I understood why I was always rejected when applying for a professional job. Even when a working position was advertised with "No experience necessary. Will train," some experience in the field was always required. My age also worked against me. Training usually referred to a much younger crowd. However, the most unskilled and inexperienced applicants lacking marketability elsewhere can find employment in retail and receive immediate compensation based on the number of hours worked. It's a way of earning money quickly and honestly. Sadly, retail also locks its employees at an income level that cannot keep up with the rising cost of living.

My first retail job was truly accidental. As I was walking with my children through a small outdoor mall, my son said, "Mom, look! They're hiring here!" There was a "Hiring" sign posted on the front window of Linens 'n Things. The following day, after taking my children to school, I walked into Linens 'n Things with my worthless resume to inquire about its job openings. The staffing agency had lowered my expectations, but hadn't crushed my spirit.

Richard, the store manager, came immediately to the front of the store and greeted me with a friendly smile. He checked my resume, which didn't seem to affect him negatively. After a brief conversation, he asked one of his five managers, specifically Brenda, the Bath manager, to interview me. It was my first interview in the world of retail, one that was going to be followed by numerous other ones, over the course of 20 years. I indicated my interest in a sales position in the Kitchen area. Brenda didn't promise anything. She gave me some general information for new employees and explained the store dress code: black or beige slacks and a white shirt. The store was going to give me a red apron. A couple of days later, I was offered a part-time cashier position with a pay of $7.50/hour. Richard needed a cashier and he knew that I wasn't ready for a sales position. I had no sales experience, which is crucial in a successful sales department.

How did I get hired as a cashier without experience? Richard usually placed college students or applicants with a college education in cashier positions, even if they lacked experience. He believed that it was a sensitive job with financial complexities affecting the business. Not all stores value college education. In 2009, after Linens 'n Things had closed nationwide, I was interviewed for a cashier position at Target. My interviewer asked me why I was pursuing employment in retail although I had college degrees. She thought I was overqualified and I had better options. She didn't hire me, but she taught me to minimize my college education in my resume, generally removing anything above my Bachelor's Degree. In reality, I didn't have better employment options.

Although the pay was low, Richard had given me a gift. A cashier position in a very busy store, like Linens 'n Things in La

Jolla, CA, was an opportunity to learn customer service and gain general business experience. I accepted my first cashier position as a temporary job, hoping to find something better. Unknowingly, I was going to be channeled into lifetime retail employment. One job was going to lead to another one, enriching my resume with a variety of positions and tasks that increased my ability to get hired quickly. I learned something useful from all the companies I worked for, including the bad ones, regardless of the amount of training that they provided. Profitable companies consistently offered me quality training.

I worked in a variety of different retail businesses either as a cashier or a salesperson. My pay didn't quite double over a period of 20 years. It allowed me to live and raise my children, although requiring constant family assistance and loans. I'm still not able to pay for my rent alone. Rent, car insurance, utility bills, food and necessities keep increasing in price year after year. My ex-husband stopped paying court-ordered alimony many years ago. My father's help also ended years ago, when he passed away. I live with my daughter, who has a professional full-time job and owns a house. Like many people in retail, I worked for years to guarantee the survival and well-being of my children and myself. I am now 71 years old. My daughter provides a house in which I can live. I have been working to pay for food and take care of some household bills, enabling my daughter to save money. She should never end up in the desperate economic situations of my past. Not all retail employees are as lucky as I am. Many of them don't have a supporting family. They are on their own with children to raise, rents to pay, chronic illnesses, and nothing in their bank. Most of them live paycheck to paycheck.

Retail employees figure out how to survive on a low pay. They may receive supplemental income, they share apartments with others, or, like I did, they receive help from relatives. Brenda, the Bath manager, was a divorced, middle-aged woman, who lived with her parents. She explained to me that she couldn't afford to pay rent on her salary. California rents were and probably still are disproportionate to the income of retail workers. Paula, a middle-aged woman responsible for most of the store displays, was married to an engineer, but needed additional income to pay her bills.

All employees constantly tried to improve their salary, moving from business to business. The first head-cashier I met at Linens 'n Things was a young man who left the company to join the Navy. He was excited because, as he told me, the Navy was going to pay for his housing and education, which no part-time retail job could have done for him. The next head cashier was finishing her Master's Degree in Business. She left Linens 'n Things to accept a full-time business job elsewhere. She was replaced by another student finishing her Master's Degree, who left the company to accept a full-time teller position at Wells Fargo Bank. Ken, a young journalist, wasn't earning enough money with his freelance articles, published on *The San Diego Union-Tribune*. He resigned his cashier position at Linens 'n Things to work as a receptionist with higher pay for one of the interior decorators that shopped in our store.

When you walk into a store and encounter a salesperson that greets you with a beautiful smile and engages you into a humorous conversation, don't be deceived by appearances. That salesperson is putting on a show. A good show leads to a good sale. Behind the smile, there is usually financial struggle. Often there is also a large amount of human struggle in these employees' lives. One of the cashiers working at Linens 'n Things was married to an alcoholic man, who worked only occasionally. Once, I found her crying in the break room, although a few minutes earlier she had been greeting customers with a smile. One of the salespersons at Neiman Marcus had been freed from a physically abusive marriage. Eventually her ex-husband had died, but at a fairly advanced age, this woman was still working to pay her mortgage and keep afloat. All retail employees generally carry a heavy load of existential grief, but they wake up each day, ready to greet everyone with a warm smile and a positive attitude.

Retail requires psychological stability and strong physical stamina to stand for many hours each day, year after year. Like everyone else, I developed spider web veins on my legs. Many employees start experiencing pain in their knees and hips, sometimes leading to knee replacements and other types of surgeries. It's hard work for low pay. Everyone has problems and no one has enough money to live comfortably. However, retail employees tend to be mentally strong individuals. They have to cope with their own difficulties while, at the same time, they are constantly solving their customers' problems.

Experienced salespersons, in particular, are very cool-headed. They listen attentively to their customers and remain calm at all times. External factors don't affect their emotions. If you insult a successful salesperson, you will receive an empty stare and no apparent reaction. In one of the timeshare companies where I worked briefly, we listened to taped phone calls as part of our training. In one of them, an angry customer voiced her rightful complaints. One of the most common problems was the inability to access specific resorts which were always booked up much in advance. The company didn't have enough resorts to accommodate the number of customers acquiring timeshares. The experienced salesperson listening to the angry customer would frequently interject "My Goodness!" This had a slightly calming effect on the customer who felt that a company representative was listening. At the same time, the salesperson asked relevant questions to gather information leading to the identification of a problem that could be solved with the sale of additional timeshares. Experienced salespersons never take customers' anger, frustration, or insults personally. They turn a negative into another sale, if possible. When I confront an upset customer, even if I no longer work as a salesperson, I still hear myself saying "My Goodness!" repetitively. It keeps me disengaged from the crisis and it psychologically helps the customer feel comfortable.

Neiman Marcus is the retail store that paid me the most and offered me a full-time job at the time of hiring. This company didn't seem to care about its employees' age. It established a yearly sales goal for each employee, which increased each year. If an employee didn't meet this goal, the company gave a warning to the employee. Six months later, if the sales goal hadn't been reached, the company laid off that salesperson. Sales goals were all that mattered. Employees could keep their sales job indefinitely, regardless of their age, as long as they were successful. One of the oldest salespersons I met there was a very nice man in his 80's who worked in the Beauty department. He was very knowledgeable and had many customers. After a couple of heart attacks, he retired, but Neiman Marcus would have kept him longer, if he had wanted to stay.

There is a widespread belief that if you're going to work in retail, you'd better be a manager. The pay is higher, you receive more benefits, and most of all your position is safer. Wrong! Managers don't always receive a higher salary and they don't always have a safer job. At Neiman Marcus, a long-time, top salesperson in the store explained to me that he didn't want to become a manager although the store would have liked him to be a manager. With his commissions, he was earning a higher salary than a manager.

Due to his high sales, the store allowed him to have an office where he could meet with his customers or actually sit for part of the day to contact them. He also taught me that, when on vacation (which wasn't mandatory, but strongly encouraged), he earned more money than when he was in the store. In addition to their hourly salary, salespersons on vacation received an average of their yearly commissions, which adds up significantly over a period of two weeks. Managers' positions weren't safe. The corporate office laid off managers easily in times of crisis, but didn't touch the jobs of successful salespersons who were bringing in money for the company on a regular basis. Managers were replaceable. Successful salespersons were not. Every good salesperson at Neiman Marcus knew that and didn't worry about lay-offs.

Full-time employees do have better economic protection than part-time employees. They have permanent contracts and their working hours remain fairly constant, whereas a part-time employee's hours can be cut abruptly. At Walmart, during slow months, the part-time employees' hours are usually reduced. My hours dropped from about 32-35 hours to as low as 23 once. Unlike full-time employees in some other companies, full-time cashiers at Walmart don't receive paid vacation days. Just like part-time employees, they have to request days off, preferably up to six months in advance, and hope that these days are approved. If they are granted, employees financially cover as many days off as they can using hours accrued working. Otherwise, their days off remain unpaid.

Part-time employees can be fired at any time, without reason and without notice. They really have no protection. In 2010, while working at Lord & Taylor in Boca Raton, FL, I saw how easily a part-time worker can lose employment. Lord & Taylor had just opened the Boca Raton store in October 2010 and valued customer service very highly. The store was filled with snowbirds from the northeast who were very familiar with Lord & Taylor and expected to be treated the same way they were usually treated in New York. If unsatisfied, they threatened to complain at the corporate level. The managers didn't want complaints at the corporate office. In December, a seasonal employee upset a customer who didn't contact the corporate office, but went straight to the general manager's office. The employee was called into the manager's office and ten minutes later was gone. She never came back. Customers always win in a reputable store. They can be difficult, but they can also become the employees' best allies.

I was fired once, in 2015, while working as a part-time cashier at Sears in Orlando, FL. I was in my two-week training period. As the computer training couldn't be completed due to constant glitches in the system, my hiring manager told me to get as much experience as I could on the register. Sadly, my hiring manager was never around. Samantha, one of the managers in the clothing department, didn't really want me to learn closing tasks. During closing time, she used to send me to hang clothes back on the racks rather than allowing me to understand the register closing procedures, which are different in every store. As I had been a cashier for a long time, I decided to work around these restrictions and still managed to understand my responsibilities in bits and pieces. On my last day of employment, Samantha sent me to work on the register with Luke, who claimed to be a supervisor. He didn't allow me to ring up customers. He told me to complete my computer training on the computer near the register. I struggled the entire time on the freezing computer, getting very little done. When a long line of customers formed, I immediately rushed to one of the registers, but Luke stopped me.

"No, I'll take care of the customers. Go back to the computer!" he said.

I suspected that he was definitely not a supervisor because no supervisor in America would allow customers to stand in line, when avoidable. However, I was new and obedient, and I followed his lead. When Luke went on his lunch hour, I was finally able to ring up customers and get some experience. He returned almost two hours later and told me that the managers wanted to see me. The managers he was referring to turned out to be Samantha and the manager of the Appliances department, with whom I had never dealt before. They placed some paperwork in front of me to sign, telling me that I was fired.

"Why are you firing me?" I asked.

"Because no one likes you here."

I hadn't broken any rule, I hadn't made any mistake, I had followed all orders and procedures. Most of all, I had worked for the company for ten days, without completing my training period. And yet, they had the ability to terminate my employment simply because, as they stated, they didn't like me. I still wonder today why they didn't like me, as I hardly interacted with any of them and just concentrated on my tasks. My firing paperwork didn't indicate any reason for my loss of employment. I went home realizing how vulnerable part-time employees really are. It was a very difficult situation for me because I had just recovered from a kneecap fracture that had required two surgeries and loans to survive. I needed to get back to work and fast.

A manager has absolute power over his/her employees. A bad manager can be very damaging. The good news is that over a period of 20 years, I encountered many excellent managers in every store. Most managers, especially long-time, experienced managers are usually very good. They train their employees to help them succeed and to allow the business to flourish. They set an example with their demeanor and they teach valuable information, from ways of handling a variety of situations that pop up during the course of the day, to *CYA* (Cover Your Ass), as one of my best Walmart managers taught me early in my employment. Yes, *CYA* is a very important lesson to be learned. Each time a situation that can threaten a regular company procedure arises, one should never break the rules or create new rules. At Linens 'n Things, Lauren, the Kitchen department manager, was fired after working for the company for a long time. Michael, the operations manager told me that she had been fired for not following procedures correctly. In another company, a long-time operational manager was fired by the corporate office because he had signed a paper he had no authority to sign. He must have become comfortable in his position and assumed that he could cut corners. As Paula taught me, one should never take a job for granted.

"I have to prove myself every day," she told me once.

I started my shifts at 8 in the morning, although the store opened at 10 a.m. to the public. Richard allowed me to leave earlier than he would have liked, in order for me to pick up my children at school. School started at 7:30 a.m. I got up at 4:45 a.m., got ready, helped my children get ready, cooked breakfast, packed the children's lunches, and drove the children to school, which required a 25-minute car ride. The San Diego school system supplied buses only for children enrolled in special programs outside of their boundaries. After dropping my children off, I drove directly to the store to start my shift.

During the first two hours, I worked with other employees to stock the store. When we had to lift boxes off the conveyor belt, in order to move the merchandise from the truck to the store, I left the heavy ones to other employees. In spite of that, I always had a sharp pain in one of my shoulders. Paula and Sharon were able to carry huge, heavy boxes apparently with no effort. At 10 a.m., I started cash handling. If I had a slow moment, I folded towels, refilled shelves near the registers, priced merchandise, or set up a sales table following Richard's specific instructions. Occasionally, I also cleaned floors, counters, and bathrooms. My low pay never reflected the amount of work I did, but it was justified by the information I was learning in all aspects of the business.

The Linens 'n Things POS (point of sale) system I used in La Jolla in 2005 wasn't as sophisticated as many systems used today. It required a large amount of manipulation and frequent managers' approvals. Initial training consisted of basic register instructions in a training mode, as customary. However, many steps to be followed weren't in the training. Usually, head cashiers helped new cashiers learn these steps. Linens 'n Things required physical checking of IDs to process all checks and credit cards. After I moved to Florida, in 2011, my first job was a cashier position at Victoria's Secret. I started checking IDs prior to processing credit cards, as I had been doing in La Jolla, but my Victoria's Secret manager stopped me.

"You don't need to check ID for credit cards. We have an insurance company," he said.

He just wanted to move the line quickly. We had long lines of customers at Linens 'n Things too, but the cashiers were expected to be fast and thorough. On a busy day, during the holiday season, there were six to eight people in line at each of the five registers.

The head cashier was in charge of the customer service desk and was authorized to do returns. The head cashier was also responsible for posting schedules next to each register and making sure that each register counter had the necessary equipment, from pens to the latest discount information. The managers distributed pictures or physical descriptions of customers who had defrauded other stores. In one instance, a gang of thieves stole expensive Nate Berkus bath items and then returned them in another store, without receipt. Our store had no cameras and I assume that all Linens 'n Things stores had no cameras, allowing expert thieves to act with ease. Whenever a thief was clearly identified by a witness, the store manager sent an alert to all other stores in the area, with a physical description or a picture of this person. We kept this information under the counter, like a wanted poster. I never saw anyone who matched the descriptions given to me, which was probably lucky.

Whenever a suspicious return (such as the return of a Nate Berkus bath item with no receipt) was requested, cashiers had to call the manager on duty and often, the person trying to do the return ran out of the store. On one occasion, Lauren, the Kitchen manager, refused to process the return of stolen merchandise. The customer physically attacked her. The store called the police and the customer was arrested. We were taught never to confront anyone because customers with bad intentions could have been armed. One of the Linens 'n Things managers told me that in a different store, he had heroically chased a thief in the parking lot and retrieved stolen merchandise. The store had reproached him for putting himself in danger, but had also given him a pay raise.

Like all newly hired employees, I was on a learning curve. I had never used a register before and I was afraid of making mistakes. Linda, our Bedding manager, sensed my discomfort and reassured me.

"There is nothing that you can do incorrectly on this register that I cannot fix." The pressure was off.

My Linens 'n Things managers were all very good. They gave me the tools to succeed and always supported me. Our store had amazing teamwork. When I called a manager using the intercom, the manager arrived within a few seconds. If I called a salesperson to check a price or other information about a product to be returned, that salesperson would also arrive within a few seconds. One day we lost power, but we continued to process transactions with pen and paper. The managers placed flashlights throughout the store. One person filled out receipts manually. Another person calculated tax and discounts with a calculator. A manager supervised the entire front store operations, and another employee helped with bagging. In 2012, while I was working at Swim 'n Sport in Boca Raton, FL, our register didn't work for almost a week. Most of the time, I was alone during my shifts. Without the help of a team, I had to fill out orders and receipts with a pen, work out split tender transactions with a pen, call for credit card and check clearances, use the calculator to calculate tax and change to be given to the customers. My previous experience without power was extremely helpful.

All Linens 'n Things cashiers were on the line for super accuracy. All signed credit card receipts had to be placed inside the register. After the hiring of a young college student as a new cashier, I noticed during my shifts that credit card receipts were left outside of the register, under the counter. The new cashier was messy. He lost his job within a very short time. A couple of years after I started working at Linens 'n Things, Richard hired a retired See's Candies manager as a cashier. She had extensive retail experience. The new cashier was a very nice lady who never quite understood how to process coupons correctly. Richard didn't fire her, but she was denied a pay raise the following year. As in all stores, annual raises amounted to less than 50 cents per hour, but we all liked to receive our raise.

In 2006, Richard promoted me to the position of head cashier. The truck driver who brought merchandise to our store twice a week, walked in front of my register and complimented me.

"I heard you're moving up," he said.

I was dumbfounded because my pay hadn't changed with this promotion. I was just allowed to do more operations on the register and I never thought of this promotion as "moving up." In fact, I never even thought of it as a promotion. Today, 20 years later and many companies later, I understand Richard's viewpoint. The position of head cashier wasn't for everyone. We had customers who returned and repurchased multiple items applying a variety of coupons and our POS system wasn't extremely sophisticated. Richard wanted to make sure that cashiers were fully trained in all aspects of payments and customer service before touching customers' personal accounts. As a head cashier, I had mailing orders to process. We had decorators who bought large amounts of merchandise with a special discount. We had tax-free purchases fairly often. All these transactions are processed very quickly today, but years ago, they used to require special paperwork and managers' approvals. Being at the customer service desk as a head cashier, I also had unhappy customers returning merchandise who had to be treated with careful attention. Richard strongly believed in satisfying all customers. For this reason, managers satisfied the most outrageous requests.

One day, a customer walked into the store with a two-year-old, dirty toilet brush demanding its replacement because it was broken. He told me that he had no receipt and that he had already replaced the brush once, two years earlier. With a seraphic smile on my face, I called the manager on duty. I thought the customer was out of his mind, but I was already learning to be cool-headed in all situations. After a brief conversation with the customer, the manager on duty authorized the replacement of the brush. The customer left very satisfied and convinced that he could have replaced his toilet brush until he died. The important lesson was to make sure that the customers were happy and coming back to the store, which they did. A small loss is nothing as compared to a greater gain. In 2013, a similar situation happened at Lord & Taylor where a man showed up with a used Spanx underwear with no tag. He did have a receipt. He said that his wife wasn't happy with the fit. He denied that the item had been worn claiming that the item was in its dirty condition when it was purchased. The manager insisted that our store didn't sell dirty Spanx without a tag, but ultimately processed the return. As soon as the customer left, she looked at me and said, "They are pigs!" I was speechless and remembered the dirty toilet brush of Linens 'n Things, but I understood the concept of returning an item to satisfy an unhappy customer, even if taking a loss.

Although I was a cashier at Linens 'n Things, I started placing some sales. Occasionally, if there weren't enough salespersons, I would assist a customer asking for help, leaving my register just for a few minutes. I sold a large painting once and a bar table on clearance. The sale of the bar table made Richard very happy because the table was expensive even on clearance.

When a customer wanted to use a coupon that required a minimum purchase amount, but the total was a penny short, the customer had to buy an additional item to be able to use the coupon. Unlike our competitor Bed Bath & Beyond, we didn't forgive that penny. We had a variety of low-priced items displayed near the register. Although gourmet lollipops were particularly popular, customers often decided to buy something useful like a pricey cleaning product. The addition of purchases at the register to allow usage of coupons must have been significant on a nationwide scale. The price of many items seemed to be planned to be a penny short in order to increase sales.

Like all companies, Linens 'n Things wanted customers to use its store credit card in order to avoid paying interchange fees and strengthen customer loyalty. The use of a store credit card promotes repeated sales, as shown statistically. The Linens 'n Things credit card wasn't very difficult to sell as compared to other ones I encountered later, but at the time I wasn't trained to sell. I watched Lauren, the Kitchen department manager, offer a store credit card to a customer and I thought she was very convincing. If customers asked for something they weren't entitled to, she was always able to refuse with a smile and a reasonable explanation, leaving the customers happy. I decided to emulate her. I worked out a sales pitch of my own. The Linens 'n Things credit card was actually quite good. In addition to a 20% discount on the initial purchase, it offered other excellent benefits, such as two free gifts a year (nice gifts like a good quality entrance mat), and additional rewards available to cardholders only. This card was easy to sell.

As soon as I finished scanning all the items to be purchased, I made eye contact with the customer and, carefully using the wording I had perfected, I asked if he or she wanted to open "an account" with the store. I never called it a "credit card" because the mention of a credit card elicited an instant rejection. However, the customers knew it was a credit card because I gave them written information. I also asked them to fill out and sign an application form. The pitch worked. If I changed the wording even slightly, the customer rejected the card. I started opening seven or eight credit card accounts a day. After a customer said "yes," frequently the next two people in line, who had heard my pitch, also started filling out applications before I even scanned the items in their carts. Linda, the Bedding manager, questioned whether my credit card success was due to the exact words I used or due to the way I delivered them. Today, I think that the choice of words was absolutely critical, although other factors, such as the benefits of the card, came into play.

In every store I worked for, I had to figure out the exact words to sell credit cards or a required add-on item. At Swim 'n Sport, employees were supposed to add a bathing suit rinse to their sale. Initially, I was quite unsuccessful, although I tried different methods. One day, Gloria, the store manager, who had been watching me offer the rinse, said:

"Stop asking them to buy the rinse! Just tell them how to use it!"

I realized that the sale of a tangible object has to be described in its function and possibly demonstrated. I perfected my rinse pitch. After ringing up all bathing suits, towels, covers, hats and more, I made eye contact with the customer holding the rinse in my hand and I explained how to use it.

"If you put about an ounce of this rinse into a bowl full of water and you let your bathing suit soak, not only..." which was similar to "If you open an account with Linens 'n Things, not only you receive..." The first benefit was the most important one, but it was important to highlight multiple benefits, disregarding the main one as a given. Amazingly, it worked most of the time.

The most difficult credit card I had to sell was the Neiman Marcus credit card. During my job interview, my hiring manager Lisa, indicated that I would receive $10 for each account opened. It was a very large amount of money because most stores paid $5, if not less. When I told my daughter that Neiman Marcus paid $10 for each opened credit card, she immediately commented:

"They must be very difficult to sell."

She was right. The Neiman Marcus credit card didn't offer an immediate discount on the first purchase. It gave points to be accumulated and redeemed for gift cards in the future. Neiman Marcus required the opening of only two credit cards per month and it wasn't easy. The Lord & Taylor credit card was fairly easy to sell, not only because of its intrinsic benefits, but also because I was selling it in Boca Raton where the store had just reopened, after closing in Florida about 10 years earlier. Lord & Taylor had many loyal customers in the South who were thrilled by the return of one of their favorite stores. If a mother and daughter were shopping together, occasionally they both opened an account as they were extremely excited by the idea of each possessing their own Lord &

Taylor credit card. For years, if I had trouble placing a sale, I always remembered Gloria's tip "Tell them how to use it!" She was the daughter of a tuxedo salesman, who loaded the merchandise in his car and drove it to the stores. She had business in her blood and exceptional manager's skills.

My best credit card sales record at Linens 'n Things was 13 in one day. I was never able to beat or repeat this record. Like most sales, credit card sales usually slowed down in February and picked up in the summer, peaking during the holiday season. During my first year at Linens 'n Things, I won a $50 gift card in a national credit card competition held by the company. They eliminated this contest the following year. However, I still have a very good memory of my gift card award. It really made me feel good to be rewarded so lavishly. Linda insisted that I should be moved to sales. Richard wanted me on the register. I'm glad that they never moved me to sales because salespersons received no commission and I was comfortable working as a cashier.

Over the years, I learned to never do a salesperson's job when cashiering. There is no incentive and no reward in doing it. At Walmart, I watched cashiers fight over customers as if they were going to gain anything by scanning someone's items. One of the long-time cashiers used to constantly complain that another cashier always took her customers. The longer employees work in the same environment, the more territorial rights they acquire and expect. Some long-time cashiers monopolized specific registers, although registers weren't assigned. They even set up and left their personal items at that register. For the long-time cashier, getting customers was a way of expressing her territorial control. It was incongruous because cashiers don't gain sales and commission in a specific territory.

Like most part-time employees, I tried to find a better paying job. Since I had two children at home, I wasn't looking for a second job yet. After my children went to college, looking for a second job became a constant and difficult search for me. Finding two jobs that aren't in conflict with each other and that have a compatible schedule happens rarely. But at that time, a better paying part-time job in or out of retail was my goal. Since multiple head cashiers had been hired by local banks, I started applying for several part-time bank teller positions. The banks paid $11/hour for an entry level position. I went through several interviews. I received two-full time offers from Bank of America and Citibank within the same week. Throughout the interviews, no one ever mentioned a full-time job. In fact, during the Bank of America group interview, the interviewer talked about part-time shifts. Sadly, I couldn't accept those two full-time jobs, which were very good. The Citibank recruiter clearly explained that the bank closed to the public at 6:30 p.m., but I would have left around 7:00 p.m. after completing closing procedures. The school "6-to-6 program" ended at 6:00 p.m. and I still would have had an additional 25 minute drive to reach my children's school. My son probably wouldn't have even started his homework, as he worked well only in the comfort of his home. Hiring a babysitter was out of the question as I was trying to raise my pay. I had to look for a part-time job elsewhere.

I became certified to work as Clerk I and Clerk II in the San Diego City School District. I found a job as Clerk-Typist I in my children's old elementary school. The hiring representative told me that she could guarantee my job only until the end of the school year. It was November 2007 and the San Diego City School District probably already knew that, due to the recession, budget cuts were going to start soon. I received a magnificent $10.82/hour. I was finally out of retail. I no longer worked on weekends and holidays. I had a job that allowed me to sit most of the time at a desk and if the economic situation allowed it, I might have been able to be promoted. Most of all, I had good medical and dental insurance. It was a good work situation, but not for long.

In June 2008, brutal state budget cuts on education started. All new part-time employees like me were laid off immediately. Full-time employees were transferred to very distant locations, probably to encourage resignations. At this early stage of budget cuts, only regular teachers were safe. A year later, teachers were laid off too. The attendance clerk who had been with the school for 20 years, was transferred to a distant school. She told me she was going to resign. The Principal and the Vice Principal were also transferred. The school Principal resigned. The Vice Principal who was young, had a child and a non-working husband, accepted the transfer. The senior clerk, who was my direct trainer and supervisor, was also transferred to a distant location. She didn't resign because she was raising a grandchild, still in middle school. The Court of California had assigned this girl to her, because her son and daughter-in-law weren't able to take care of the child. I had a lot of respect for this old woman who was raising her granddaughter alone with devotion. In my children's school, over a period of months, most employees were laid off, including the school librarian and the front office representative, who had been there for many years and took care of many responsibilities besides greeting people.

I was jobless and, clearly, my only option was to go back into retail. I went to Linens 'n Things to make a small purchase, trying to decide how to reapply. To my surprise, Richard came up to me.

"We missed you here," he said.

I understood that he must have been dissatisfied with his new cashier. I told him I had been laid off.

"Come back at the end of August. I can hire you then," he said. I had left Linens 'n Things with a pay of $8.46/hour and I was rehired with a pay of $9/hour. Did Richard know that the store was going to close in December of that year? Probably not, even though the signs of the recession already permeated all aspects of daily life.

Store business continued with good traffic. There were only two cashiers. I was the head cashier. One major change was the constant presence of a manager in the front of the store. He stood most of the day next to the registers, monitoring business and intervening if required. I never found out what had happened in the store during my absence, but something must have elicited this change. Having a manager nearby was actually a convenience. We constantly needed approvals on the register and the manager could step in very quickly. Linda left. She had been competing with Michael for a promotion. Richard favored Michael, possibly because, years earlier, Richard had talked him into leaving Toys "R" Us to join Linens 'n Things. Linda was very driven and didn't like to be left behind. She became the store assistant manager at Victoria's Secret. Although no one knew it, she was the real winner because she was leaving the company on time. Suddenly, in October 2008, Linens 'n Things announced its bankruptcy and the closure of all its stores.

2

'Tis the Season

Watching a business reach the end of its lifespan is devastating. It's difficult to acknowledge the fact that the place where everyone invested a large amount of time and energy each day, will no longer exist and all its employees will be displaced. Our managers claimed that the Linens 'n Things store in La Jolla had always been and was still profitable. The last phase of our work in the store consisted of processing liquidation sales. The merchandise sold at a very fast pace as prices kept dropping. During the last month, a rug company rented part of the floor space and my job included the processing of rug sales, which were quite successful.

The managers reminded us multiple times that the store was going to close, indirectly encouraging us to look for new employment. I decided to stay at Linens 'n Things until the end. Some employees were applying for jobs, but were getting rejected. Right before Christmas, the store was permanently closed. All employees who hadn't left the company were laid off. My father had recently died of cancer. Therefore, my family support line had also reached its end. Due to the recession, finding another job wasn't easy. Most employees applied for a job in the same shopping mall where Linens 'n Things was located, but no one was hired. Our store was replaced by Best Buy, which didn't hire any laid off employees. Was every business afraid of a Linens 'n Things curse? I tried to get hired by Victoria's Secret, but Linda said that she couldn't hire any employees laid off by Linens 'n Things. Lauren, who had been fired by Linens 'n Things many months earlier, had found a job in another store and was able to bring in Paula. She asked me if I wanted to join them, but the location of this store was too far.

Like many other laid off employees in California, I started collecting unemployment benefits. Each month, I had to fill out a form listing all the jobs I applied for indicating date, address, and outcome. I had interviews with several banks, but none of them hired me. The recruiters explained that I was competing against laid off bank employees who were already trained and experienced. Many families lost their jobs and their houses in San Diego. "Closed" signs appeared in front of many stores. Entire families were begging at street intersections, sometimes with babies sleeping in car seats on the sidewalks. Some stores had a "Hiring" sign, but when I inquired within, the managers explained that they weren't hiring at all. They said that they hadn't removed the signs yet. The manager of a deli in which I applied, told me to leave the application. He said that interviews were going to last for weeks. Weeks of interviews in the middle of the recession for a position that required making sandwiches behind a counter? They never called me for an interview, although the "Hiring" sign wasn't taken down. According to a circulating rumor, some businesses, and in particular restaurants, hired illegally and paid employees under the table.

The government unemployment website also listed open jobs. According to this website, one of the Marshalls stores had multiple open positions. I applied and went inside the store to meet the manager. He told me that the government website was wrong because Marshalls wasn't hiring at all. I kept checking the employment website of the school district. There were no job openings there. In my children's high school, where the librarian had been laid off, mothers took turns volunteering in the library so that the students could check out books. I wasn't the only one who was having a tough time. A few years later, I heard from Michael, who was working for the 99 Cents store. He told me that he had been through some emotional difficulties trying to cope with the recession. It was a big blow for him, having been a manager at Toys "R" Us and then manager of operations at Linens 'n Things. He told me that Richard was working in a sports store, but I don't know in what capacity.

I tried to search outside of retail. I earned a real estate license hoping to improve my finances. I had a broker ready to take me in a very good office that provided mentoring. The broker asked me for about $4,000 to join her team. She also told me not to expect any sales for at least a couple of months. It was totally unrealistic. I knew I had to keep looking for a retail job because it doesn't require money to start and it pays wages immediately.

Retail employees quickly learn that it's better to accept low pay that guarantees survival rather than having high aspirations that may not even materialize. Every time I left a retail job to accept an employment position that was supposed to guarantee a higher income, I ended up in a worse financial situation. I learned that not all jobs are for everyone, but retail is open to everyone. I saw young and not so young coworkers locked in retail because their medical bills or credit card bills or rents were waiting to be paid regularly.

In November 2009, Macy's West in San Diego hired me at the UTC Mall as a seasonal sales associate with a pay of $8.60/hour. The company placed me in a department that sold casual and fine dish sets, crystals, porcelain figurines, vases, cooking pans, kitchen electrics, holiday items, and more. I absolutely loved this department. When needed, I was sent to work in Lingerie, which was on the same floor. I also sold in the Bedding and Bath areas, and gained a little experience in the Children's department near Lingerie. This job gave me low pay, temporary employment, and no benefits.

Throughout the entire time I worked at Macy's, my financial situation was dramatic. As we are very passionate about the Christmas tree tradition in our family, my daughter and I wanted to buy a few of the beautiful Macy's tree ornaments. Each year we added new ornaments to our collection. I checked out the ornaments in the store, but they were too expensive for me. I had too many bills. I decided to wait until I collected a few weekly paychecks. The money for ornaments was never there. Finally, I decided to get one ornament during the after-Christmas sales. Realistically, I had no money even for one ornament. The day after Christmas, my shift started very early as the store had an exceptionally early opening for the sales. I watched the ornaments go one after another until they were all sold out. Many years later, I was going to get justice at Neiman Marcus in Orlando. During the 7-year period in which I worked in Gift Gallery, the Neiman Marcus department that sold crystals, dish sets, holiday items, and decorative products, I bought some of the most beautiful tree ornaments one could dream of, at exceptional sale prices, with my 30% employee discount on top.

Macy's West not only provided excellent training, but had excellent managers. They were polite, intelligent, witty, and efficient. When called by phone, they always showed up in less than a minute and solved all problems with no fuss. My first manager vanished within a week, as he was transferred to another store in Los Angeles. On my first day of work, he gave me a tour of the department and spent an hour training me on the features and differences of all cookware materials and brands. He clearly loved cooking and showed a genuine interest in cookware, providing very useful training. After he left, I was assigned to another manager who was a ghost. However, if I needed help, other managers arrived to assist me and they were all outstanding.

Macy's had storage rooms on all floors. It took some experience to know which floor to go to in order to retrieve an item. It also took some experience to suggest items to the customers, due to the large variety of products we were selling. I had very limited sales experience. I was riding on instinct and customer service.

Having been in charge of the customer service desk at Linens 'n Things, I knew which appliance brands were returned more or less frequently and why. Therefore, I used my knowledge of kitchen electrical appliances. If a customer asked me which coffee maker was better or which brands I would recommend and why, I had the information and I could give suggestions. What worked against seasonal employees was the attitude of the full-time employees. We were taking their sales. They never helped me if I asked questions. They seemed to permanently occupy specific registers in busy areas, although registers weren't assigned to anyone. Lucinda didn't like anyone to use the register close to the kitchen area. On one occasion, her shift started after mine. I was on her favorite register and I had six or seven customers in line.

"I'm sorry, but I have to close this register for a while," she told me.

It made no sense, but as I felt like a guest in that department, I immediately left taking all customers with me.

"Please follow me to another register! This one is being shut down," I told them.

The customers obediently followed me to another unused register on the same floor. Ten minutes later, when I walked back to the kitchen area, I saw Lucinda standing next to her favorite register, open for business.

Lucinda must have had high sales goals and didn't like to lose sales of expensive electrics. One day, as I was selling a De Longhi espresso machine, she interrupted me.

"Do you need help with this De Longhi?" she asked me.

It seemed unusual for her to offer help. She never even replied when I greeted her. Having owned and used an electric espresso machine for years while residing in Europe, I knew how the product worked. I quickly dismissed her and closed my sale alone. She was probably trying to take my sale and she was breaking the number one rule, which is never to interrupt an ongoing sale.

At Macy's, I didn't have time to become truly proficient. As the weeks passed, I reached my goals and exceeded them only slightly. However, while working there, I realized how much I loved handling dish sets, porcelain figurines, vases and all the wonderful decorative products that I was going to sell in Gift Gallery at Neiman Marcus, years later.

When I sold my first Macy's credit card, I learned that Macy's paid cash upfront rather than adding the credit card commissions on my paycheck. The idea of putting cash in my pocket made me feel very uncomfortable after working for over three years in the very strict cashiering environment of Linens 'n Things. I actually stopped offering these cards. I opened them very rarely and I refused to ask for my commission. It was a mistake because I'm sure that the company was monitoring how many credit cards employees were opening.

In spite of the recession, sales seemed to be going well. We had a pile of artificial Christmas trees that sold out quickly. Customers came in looking for gifts, dish sets, glassware, kitchenware. One day, a woman wearing shabby and ripped clothes, with unkempt hair and no make-up, was standing in front of the fine dish sets. None of the regular employees approached her, probably assuming that she was too poor to buy anything. I greeted her just like any other customer and started a conversation. She told me that she needed a special gift, but she didn't know what she was looking for. As I was very inexperienced, I didn't ask enough questions to narrow down the options. I just randomly showed her a variety of decorative items, but she wasn't satisfied. She asked for something with a higher price. I continued to show more expensive products, wondering if she would have been able to afford them. Suddenly, I was called to the register to ring up another customer.

The shabby lady continued to roam around with no assistance. Finally, she approached me and asked to purchase one of the expensive Lladro porcelain figurines that Macy's kept locked behind glass, which I had casually shown to her without much hope. I had to call a manager to open the glass case to retrieve the object. It was a very good lesson for me: one should never judge a customer based on appearance. Making assumptions on a customer's spending ability is a rookie mistake. During my seasonal employment at Macy's West, I sold multiple Lladro figurines. I really didn't know what I was selling. I was lucky and I was very outgoing, approaching customers and showing products I didn't know much about. It was a timid introduction to my future sales of very expensive and large sculptures at Neiman Marcus.

Macy's permanent employees had the habit of greeting customers and then moving away, without establishing any rapport with them. Ten minutes later, they returned hoping that the customer was holding a product ready to be purchased. The customer seemed to belong to the first greeter, even if that employee hadn't worked on the sale. Territorial dynamics were very different in other stores. During my training at Lord & Taylor, the manager stressed that simply greeting a customer didn't give us a customer. We were expected to greet all customers we crossed in the store. They became our customers when we assisted them. At Neiman Marcus, territories became even more complicated because most customers had regular salespersons.

"Sorry, but I only shop with Paul," they would tell the employee who attempted to start a sale.

Before going to the store, customers usually texted their favorite salesperson to check if he or she was working that day. If their favorite salesperson wasn't in the store, the customers often asked to have their purchase rung up for the absent salesperson. Customer loyalty was very strong at Neiman Marcus. Salespersons did a tremendous amount of work to satisfy their regular customers. The customers could depend on them to be well informed and to have many problems solved. Often, they made purchases by phone, without even walking into the store.

My seasonal job at Macy's ended at the end of the first week of January 2010. I started collecting unemployment benefits and looking for a job again. In the spring, a full-time position opened at Macy's in the same department and store where I had worked as a seasonal employee. My interview was confirmed online the night before, but when I reached the store, I was told that the position had already been filled a week earlier.

Finally, in November 2010, I was hired by See's Candies as a seasonal sales associate. Since the holiday season was always very busy for See's Candies, the store called in retired employees as seasonal associates. However, they weren't enough for the expected holiday traffic. For this reason, a few additional employees like me were added. Working at See's Candies was like stepping into another century. The retired old ladies in their long white uniforms walking into the store to do their shifts added character. I felt that Mrs. See was going to pop up at any moment.

The See's Candies 1930's signature lab coat was probably the most difficult uniform I was ever asked to wear. The small size was too tight and the medium was very long below my knees and wide around my entire body. I kept the length, but I had to take in the sides because it really looked like a sack. The uniform did project the identity of the store. It was a costume. Selling is putting on a show. Voice, motions, appearance all work together to close the sales. It's theater at its best.

Our day of work was preceded by mandatory physical exercises in the back of the store. We had to stretch and bend for about 20 minutes to prepare for our shift. Employees were allowed to eat as many chocolates as they wanted, as long as they logged each eaten candy in a sheet posted on the wall. They had to enter the number and type of chocolates they ate, and the date of consumption. That was enough to curb my appetite for candy. Since we prepared bags of candies to be sold, some of the employees nonchalantly chewed multiple chocolates with gusto, as they weighed them and placed them in the clear plastic bags. I don't believe that they were planning to enter the information in any sheet.

In 2010, the See's Candies store where I worked had a very archaic POS system. Nothing could be scanned. Prices had to be memorized and entered manually into the register. It was almost like working in an old mom-and-pop store. Credit cards were processed on a couple of machines connected to the register. The managers spent a long time unrolling the internal register tape all the way to the floor if they had to search for specific data.

On my first day of work, I found a problem that drew a lot of attention. The two-pound boxes of chocolates were incorrectly labeled as one-pound boxes. I realized the mistake because the products had no barcodes and we had to memorize the prices. Therefore, I checked the display table looking for the price. The assistant manager removed all two-pound boxes from the sale floor. The employees and managers in the store were shocked by this mistake and talked about it for several days.

Anyone could come into the store and ask to taste chocolates for free. Some people came into the store regularly, several times a week, to eat free chocolates without buying anything. On some days we also approached all visitors with a tray full of candies, so that they could taste them. It was an effective marketing method because See's chocolates are delicious and sell themselves due to their high quality. Yet, the sales didn't go as well as expected. I was told that in the past years, there were lines of customers that went outside the door. It never happened that year.

Several problems affected the business negatively besides the recession. The store manager was convinced that nothing had to be done to push the sales of See's Candies, because we were in a neighborhood store with regular customers. The two front windows of the store had minimal and unattractive holiday decorations that probably weren't catchy. The store prepared beautiful gift baskets with a variety of candies, but they were difficult to sell because the prices were either too high or too low. Customers were interested in the gift baskets and examined their contents. However, the high prices weren't approachable for many people in the middle of the recession. The low prices were too low for a proper gift. It would have been difficult, but possible to change the selection of products in the baskets in order to modify the overall price. I mentioned to the manager that customers seemed discouraged by the high prices of the baskets.

"That's how we do them every year," was her answer.

She expected the usual crowd of holiday shoppers, but we had a very slow holiday season. Yet, the store generously gave a box of chocolates as a gift to each employee. It was a very nice gesture in a very quaint store, at a very difficult time.

At the end of December 2010, I was unemployed again when my seasonal job ended. It was time for me to move out of California where the prices were growing and the jobs were inexistent. Since my daughter had started attending UCF in Orlando, I started organizing a move to Florida. I could give my daughter in-state tuition one year after my move. Additionally, I wasn't going to break my divorce agreement by moving out of state, since my son was also going to start college outside of California, in the fall. After an elaborate search, I picked Boca Raton. Retail had to be good there due to tourism, although the place was relatively small. Two months prior to my son's high school graduation, I was hired by Vons, a grocery store close to my residence. This is truly the only job I ever accepted without the intention of remaining with the company. Working at Vons helped me financially move out of state. Had I not relocated to Florida, I would have become homeless.

The hiring for this job was also extremely fast. Nothing like the deli that was going to consider applicants for weeks! When Vons called me for the interview, I was afraid I was going to be rejected as usual. After a series of questions, the recruiter seemed satisfied. He told me that he was going to conduct a drug test in the store and a background check on the computer and, if I passed both tests, I was hired. It was like a dream come true. He performed the drug test by leaving a large cotton swab filled with a special chemical in my mouth, for a specific amount of time. After I passed this test, he proceeded with my background check. I left the interview in a daze. Vons had hired me as a courtesy clerk for about 35 hours a week with a pay of $8.10/hour.

My job consisted of bagging for the cashier, retrieving carts for two hours each day, assisting customers to find items in the store if they asked for help, and checking the aisles for spills. Occasionally I did some stocking, although there were people hired specifically for that task. I was assigned to the store where I had shopped for ten years. I knew that store inside out. I knew where most products were and I could assist customers well. Twice, I had a mystery shopper sent by the company to check on my customer service.

Due to my familiarity with the store, I passed the tests easily. The managers were very happy with me because it was important for the store to pass these tests.

Retrieving carts was one of my favorite activities. I took off my apron, wore my sunglasses, and stepped outside into the warm, summer sun. It was pleasant to walk around the area surrounding the store. Carts had to be retrieved according to specific procedures. Depending on their location, some had to be retrieved first because if a secret shopper found more than a certain number of carts outside of the lot, the store was going to be penalized.

The working conditions at Vons were good. The store staff was extremely friendly. The managers told me that I could be promoted within the store, meaning that Vons offered opportunities for advancement. However, the timing of this job was wrong because I was already arranging my move out of state. Working in retail teaches you never to plan for the future. You live paycheck to paycheck with a very low income. You change the course of your life based on adversities that occur in the present. Poor people become daring risk takers, if necessary to survive. They live in the present, maybe without health insurance. Rich people live in the future, always planning, investing, waiting to reap benefits, and missing out on life a little. Life is like sand slipping out of your hands in between your fingers. Poor people enjoy their life one day at a time, grasping tightly what they have because they know it won't be there again.

The Vons grocery store offered "$5 Friday." Due to the recession, California families couldn't afford to go out on weekends. Therefore, Vons sold an item in each area of the store for $5. One of the managers explained that families usually rented a movie and put together a delicious and economic meal on Friday night. "$5 Friday" was a generous gesture extended to many loyal neighborhood customers going through a very difficult financial time. In this store, not only I felt I was part of a team, but also part of a tight community. Humanly, it was good.

3

Riding the Roller Coaster

Unlike California, Florida offered a variety of available jobs. As soon as we arrived in Boca Raton, I applied for multiple positions open in the Town Center Mall. The first store that hired me was Macy's. They placed me in a women's clothing area and gave me an immediate three-day schedule to be extended in the following days. However, I resigned after my first day of work. Territorial dynamics were even more difficult here than in San Diego. Miranda claimed to be the French Connection brand ambassador and monopolized one of the registers. The other saleswomen in the department said that she wasn't a brand ambassador. They all kept away from her and her register because Miranda yelled and created scenes in front of the customers. Morale was low. Several saleswomen told me that they were planning to leave Macy's for another job because sales weren't going well for them. Traffic didn't seem very good considering that the store was having sales.

One customer approached me and asked me to look for a top on sale in her size. I checked the sale display racks and, with a little luck, I found it. Then, as I was about to ring up the purchase, Miranda showed up.

"That's my customer! I'm ringing her up!" she yelled. It was quite an embarrassing situation.

"I'm not your customer! She helped me! She's ringing me up!" said the shopper, pointing at me. I completed the transaction. After the customer left, I still had to deal with Miranda's anger.

"I greeted her as soon as she arrived. She was my customer!" she said.

Greeting a customer seemed to give this saleswoman customer ownership and sales rights. I explained that the customer had asked me to look for her top, but Miranda wasn't appeased at all. The other saleswomen watched with sad resignation. They seemed to have given up on their sales in a territory that wasn't giving equal and fair opportunities to everyone. The law shaping that department was survival of the fiercest!

I had seen enough. My finances were in a very delicate predicament with both children about to start their fall semester in college. We were sleeping on the floor, on cheap inflatable mattresses that I had bought at Walgreens. Our furniture consisted of a cheap Walmart table with three chairs and a small TV. After unsuccessfully trying to sell my furniture in San Diego, I had thrown away or donated most of it, prior to my departure. The North American Van Lines sales representative had told me that his company had to significantly lower all its prices because California residents were getting stuck, as they were unable to afford their moves out of state or out of town. However, I couldn't afford the reduced price. The company quoted a very low storage price that I could handle. I left in storage our three beds and irreplaceable items. It was going to take me more than five years to be able to pay for the shipment of my boxes to Florida. Some of the boxes never arrived, although I had paid storage regularly month after month.

At the end of my first shift, I went to the Macy's Human Resources Office and resigned. I was asked if I wanted to work on call, whenever they needed to cover an absence. I turned down the offer because I needed a steady job. Luckily, I was hired almost immediately by Victoria's Secret. My daughter had also applied for a job there. In her case, it was supposed to be a summer job, meaning that she would have quit very soon to start her fall semester at UCF. We were interviewed on different days, but she didn't get hired.

Victoria's Secret hired students from the local university, who worked during the school year. The store also had some established employees, like Alicia, a middle-aged woman who had been with the company for many years and wasn't planning to leave. She knew everything about current and previous merchandise. She knew where everything was and could assist customers extremely well. I asked her why she wasn't a manager. She said that she didn't want a management position because she didn't like that type of responsibility. Alicia wanted a simple paycheck. She had financial difficulties. She lived in an apartment complex that had problems.

At one point, she was without air conditioning. Her son took care of her as much as he could. If I had any question or needed help with the merchandise, I always asked her because she was prompt and efficient. In a store with a high amount of turnover, Alicia was a precious employee.

At Victoria's Secret, employees wore 90% black clothing and a white shirt. In the "Pink" section of the store, women had to wear several layers of trending "Pink" clothes to advertise the merchandise. The environment was very casual, but conservative. No extreme hair coloring, no short or revealing clothes, no visible body piercings except for ear piercing, no nail art interfering with work were allowed. Victoria's Secret is one of the most successful businesses I worked for. Foot traffic was tremendous. I was hired to work 15 hours a week, but within a short time I had 30 hours. I was paid $8.06/hour.

Every day, one or two employees were placed in a different room to assist customers while preventing loss. The store was always crowded and theft could occur easily. Although I was hired as a cashier, I ended up working in various rooms every day, which was nice because it allowed me to learn what products we had. One day, a customer grabbed a large amount of merchandise and ran out of the store. A manager alerted security and chased the thief. In another case, a woman who had made a very large purchase, left the store and placed her Victoria's Secret bag on the floor to make a phone call. Someone grabbed her bag and ran away. She had to return to the store and purchase all her items a second time.

The end of our work day was a go-backs nightmare. We spent hours folding and separating articles by size and style on the tables and inside the drawers. The customers left piles of products everywhere. Sometimes, I drove home at midnight, although the store had closed to the public at 10 p.m. Victoria's Secret was an amazingly well-run business that attracted customers of all ages. I am glad I was part of this company, even if only for a short time.

One month after I started working at Victoria's Secret, Sandra, the store manager of Swarovski where I had also applied for a job, called me to schedule an interview. She hired me very quickly as a part-time salesperson.

"I believe that no one should work for less than $10 an hour," she told me. That was an unbelievable pay for me.

A retail worker can be hired with a pay that is higher or lower than the previous one, depending on the hiring store and wage laws. Switching jobs is like riding a roller coaster. Since multiple factors influence the selection of a new employment position, retail workers can end up with a lower hourly wage than in their previous job. Generally, they try to change job to improve their pay, but sometimes location, job type, and working conditions can be significant selection criteria as well. Yet, hourly pay remains fundamental. Sara, a salesperson in the Neiman Marcus Children's department, in Orlando, FL, told me that she had left a job to switch to an American Express position because the company was going to pay her one dollar more per hour. Considering that the annual raise in retail can amount to 20-30 cents per hour, one dollar is an extraordinary increase. Sara and I laughed about that dollar because Neiman Marcus never raised our hourly wage annually. To increase pay, we had to sell more and earn a higher commission on top of our base pay.

I'll always remember Sandra as a guardian angel. She had a very good heart and cared for her employees. She hired a young woman who had epilepsy, taking her in with some accommodations. My coworker never worked alone and she couldn't climb the ladder to retrieve merchandise from a high shelf in the stockroom. She called me whenever she needed to do so. She never had a seizure in our store. Her job was a lifesaver because she didn't seem to have anyone taking care of her. Sandra was her guardian angel also.

The Swarovski store was a triumph of glitz and sparkle. The employees felt it and the customers felt it. Each Swarovski store has a unique entrance decorated with sparkling crystals. Some customers used to describe the Swarovski stores they had visited in other countries. I was always impressed by the frequent description of the store in Amsterdam, which has entrance steps filled with crystals.

All employees wore a professional jacket. Women employees wore Swarovski earrings, bracelets, rings, and necklaces, which they bought gradually with their discount. Men also wore

Swarovski jewelry designed for men. Employees weren't allowed to wear any other type of jewelry with the exception of wedding bands and engagement rings. New collections arrived frequently. Store operations were very well organized. Training was exceptional.

Initial online training taught us company values, information about crystals, and features of different collections. We learned about the different types of crystal cuts and how some signature ones brought out the most sparkling effect possible. Like all employees working in that store, I fell in love with the products I was selling. The crystals were made in Austria, but the various collections were created in France by exceptional designers. The company tied design to business. I never lost sight of the beauty and the design while I focused on sales and customer service.

An effective technique I learned at Swarovski, which I continued to apply elsewhere afterwards, was to always leave the customers with a potential future purchase in mind. After selling and upselling anything that could be possibly added to the transaction, at the register I drew the customer's attention to an item that the customer probably liked, based on the purchase made and the previous conversation. Convinced that the sale was over, the customer paid attention without raising defensive barriers and allowed to be emotionally directed to a new point of interest. It's a technique that brings customers back into the store.

Training was ongoing as new collections arrived in the store. Initially, I felt overwhelmed by the large volume of merchandise I had to become familiar with. I was replacing an employee who had been hired by Bloomingdale's. As he was finishing his last few days of work in our store, I approached him on the subject.

"How long does it realistically take to know all these products? So many necklaces and pendants and bangles...How long does it take to learn where everything is?" I asked him.

"A couple of months," he said. I stared at him in disbelief.

Unlike crystal figurines, jewelry products weren't kept in the stockroom, in the back of the store. Every time I needed to retrieve a jewelry item, I had to identify the right drawer and then take out all the boxes until I found the correct one. It wasn't easy because the picture of the item on the box didn't always reflect its real size. A box that showed the picture of a chain with very large links, may have contained a chain with small links. Some earrings were available in various colors. In some cases, I memorized the style numbers matching different colors to quickly retrieve the right box. Bangles were in multiple drawers mixed together. One had to keep opening drawers and search until the right one turned up. Rings were even more complicated because they came in different sizes that were in multiple drawers. In reality, after a couple of months, I was able to go straight to the correct drawer and I knew where most things were.

Four months later, when a customer needed suggestions for a specific occasion, I was actually able to show a variety of options. Brides brought the picture of their dress looking for jewelry. One man asked me for an anniversary gift. After showing various options to him, he purchased a sensational set that included a necklace and earrings made with crystals and ceramic. A couple of weeks later, his wife came into the store with her friends. She had been very satisfied with her husband's choice. The group was browsing around the store. One successful sale led to more sales.

One morning, a man walked into the store in a hurry and asked for help.

"I need something for my girlfriend, but I am in a rush because my wife is shopping at Bloomingdale's," he told me.

He also indicated that he was interested in a heart. Although I felt like an accessory to a crime, I quickly showed him different heart pendants. He made his selection, but didn't want the Swarovski bag. He hid the gift in his pocket. This episode haunted me for a long time because I sadly envisioned his wife shopping at Bloomingdale's, totally clueless about her failed marriage. I had to learn to be tough. There is no room for emotions or judgement in the retail world. Sales are all that matter.

Sandra didn't get along with Barbara, the district manager. She said that Barbara was disrespectful. Barbara showed up in our store unannounced and sometimes even rang up customers on the register. She made morning opening procedures difficult. The opening employee had many tasks to perform before opening the door to the customers. I had to unlock the door, turn off the alarm, take the money to be deposited in the bank, turn the alarm back on, lock the front door and fly to the bank. Then, I had to go back to the store and listen to a very long message that Barbara left every day on the store voicemail.

I usually placed the lengthy message on speakerphone and listened to it while taking care of my tasks. Barbara's speech usually didn't convey any information of relevance that I didn't already have. However, at a certain point in her message, she inserted a request to check if the opening employee had listened to it. For example, she asked the employee to reply and give her some specific information before a set time in the morning. I had to open the registers, check email messages, print relevant information and reply to some of them, turn on lighting and music, dust the shelves, straighten price tags, clean the glass counter, and make sure that all crystals were well displayed while paying attention to Barbara's words. Customers started lining up in front of the store 15 minutes before I opened the door. After opening to the public, I wouldn't have had time to listen to Barbara's long voice message and reply to it.

Sandra was a little disorganized according to Jennifer, the full-time employee. Jennifer claimed that she had to constantly pick up after her. I thought that Jennifer was extreme, but she was probably hoping to become a manager herself one day. Initially,

Jennifer considered me as a threat to her sales. Once, she yelled at me in front of Sandra, who led her to her office and reprimanded her for lack of respect. In time, as she saw that I minded my own business and didn't interfere with her sales, Jennifer mellowed down and started accepting me. She was very accurate and very sales driven. She checked everything that everyone did in the store. One day, out of the blue, she said, "You're good." It was a phrase of acceptance, which had taken me four months to earn. Afterwards, we were able to work together harmoniously, but I always let her have control because she liked to micromanage the store. When a customer walked in with a package and asked to make a return, she would immediately route that person to me, regardless of whose turn it was to assist the next customer. A return meant spending an extraordinary amount of time to pick a different item, which Jennifer didn't like to do. Customers kept coming into the store and time was precious because we had daily sales goals.

Products that I placed on hold disappeared from the shelf, although I never got credit for them. At first, I thought that Jennifer was selling them using her employee number when I wasn't in the store. One day, I found her in the stockroom with a very somber expression.

"Carla didn't give me credit for my hold," she explained.

"How do you know?" I asked her.

"Because I talked to my customer. He came to the store to make his purchase in the evening, during Carla's shift."

He had purchased an annual Crystal Society piece. An employee earned a $25 bonus for each Crystal Society piece sold above the minimum required per month. Perhaps Carla was the person selling my holds using her number. Carla had financial problems. She was always looking for a second job to add to her Swarovski job.

Jennifer cared for her sales dearly and had been mentioned in the Swarovski national newsletter for being one of the employees who sold the Bald Eagle. At that time, it was the largest colored piece that Swarovski made with a very low number of crystal units. The Bald Eagle was a limited-edition piece, with very few left in the United States. Our store still had one eagle.

"Who is going to sell the last eagle?" Sandra would frequently write on the daily communication sheet.

"I will!" someone used to add on the side of the sheet.

"Dream on!" someone else added.

The sale of the last eagle ended in the most deflating manner. A couple entered the store during one of my shifts and the man immediately noticed the huge crystal bird. I took the masterpiece off the shelf and placed it in front of him, describing its features. The man became more and more interested.

"Don't you think that it looks beautiful? Wouldn't it look really good in the living room?" he asked his wife.

They discussed the placement of the eagle in their house and I started believing that they were going to buy it. They also discussed the high price, turning the eagle and inspecting all its sides. Suddenly, I noticed that it was missing one of its talons. It was like taking a soufflé out of the oven too soon and watching it quickly collapse. The cracked talon was still on the display shelf. We lost the sale. The crystal figurines had to be intact and Sandra had already told us that there was no possibility of getting another eagle. Who had cracked the eagle talon? The mystery remained unsolved.

Sadly, during a meeting with the district manager, Sandra left and never came back. She was replaced by Vicky. Soon afterwards, an unusual situation occurred. One of the lights on a key display shelf stopped working. Vicky told us that she was working on its replacement. It seemed to take a long time. Week after week, I had to take the items on the dark display shelf and move them onto a lit counter to show the radiance of the pieces to the customers. It was quite inconvenient. I credit Vicky with one major improvement. She reorganized the products stocked in the drawers. It became much easier to find them.

The salespersons in our store gradually left. Carla lost hours and vanished. Vicky lost the on-call helpers who came during Crystal Society events. These women had other jobs, but they all sincerely enjoyed working at Swarovski. One of them worked for her own family business. She told me that she loved buying Swarovski jewelry and was happy to use the employee discount. She used to wear beautiful Swarovski earrings, necklaces, and bracelets in the store, advertising for the company. The on-call salespersons were extremely professional and well experienced. They knew the merchandise and had dealt with Crystal Society members many times. Vicky started calling them the night before an event, without giving them the usual one week's notice. They all vanished.

Vicky didn't allow me to participate in Crystal Society events, but I managed to sell Crystal Society pieces during regular store hours. However, on more than one occasion, I had to correct Vicky because she entered into the system the wrong number of Crystal Society pieces I sold each month, which determined my bonus. Jennifer ended up in a different store. I don't know exactly how it happened. My coworker with epilepsy vanished. Vicky raised my pay to $10.20/hour, but cut my hours from 35 to 10. She was indirectly telling me to leave.

Jeremy, a salesperson in another Swarovski location came occasionally to our store to cover some hours. He used to take men's jewelry pieces from the sale displays and wear them during his shifts. We weren't supposed to wear jewelry that we hadn't purchased. Vicky was hiring very young employees to replace experienced salespeople. I wasn't as experienced as Jennifer or Carla because I had been working at Swarovski only for eight months. Yet, I met all my sales goals. During my last week of work, I reached my weekly goal on the first day.

Replacing an entire staff of experienced employees within a very short time may have backfired on Vicky after I left. The newly hired employees didn't even seem loyal to the store. One of them told me that she was planning to raise money to pay her college loans and then quit to earn her Master's Degree. Another one wore a large Betsy Johnson bangle watch instead of a Swarovski watch. Due to the large size of this noticeable bangle on her arm, she was advertising Betsy Johnson watches without realizing it. It was against the rules.

When I asked if I could have more hours, Vicky offered to let me cover a shift at Jeremy's store. Although it was my first time in a new store, I had a very good day of sales and I left an item on hold that would have allowed me to reach my daily goal. At the end of my shift, Jeremy started his shift. I told him about my hold before leaving. The customer had called to place his hold and was planning to come to the store that evening. A couple of days later, Barbara called me to inform me that a customer in Jeremy's store had reached out to her to complain about me. She didn't know the reason for the complaint nor the details. I couldn't think of any customer who had left dissatisfied. I called the other store and asked Jeremy if he had sold my hold. He said that no customer had come in to buy it. That seemed very strange because the customer had been very definite about the hold and his intentions to buy that same day. I wondered if there was any connection between the customer's complaint and my unsold hold. I was getting very tired of the drama occurring in such a magnificent company. It was time for me to look for another job with more than 10 hours a week.

In April 2012, I accepted a keyholder position at Swim 'n Sport, a ladies' designer swimwear store. I was on the roller coaster again. My pay dropped to $9.25/hour, but I had 35 hours. I still keep the crystal keychain that Sandra gave me as a Christmas holiday gift before she left the company. It has a number "1" showing through the crystal to indicate the end of my first year at Swarovski, even though I had not worked there for an entire year. I always considered this keychain as a lucky charm that had a protective power over me. It was all in my mind, but it felt good to feel protected.

Swim 'n Sport was located in Mizner Park, an exclusive shopping area of Boca Raton. Mizner Park was a difficult retail location. Many stores closed or moved elsewhere due to low traffic. It's a location that did fairly well from October to April, when snowbirds from the Northeast and Canada spent the winter in Florida. Business started to slow down in May. In the summer, on some days, no customer entered our store, during the entire course of the day. My hiring manager clearly indicated to me that upselling was extremely important in this store. At that time, an average sale totaled about $200-$250, if a customer bought only one bathing suit. If she bought two suits, the sale would rise to $450-$500, which was a fairly good sale. Therefore, we had to push cover-ups, hats, sunglasses, bags, and other accessories, as well as our add-on champion, the rinse! All these additions could raise the sale to $700-$800, which was considered a good sale.

We did have extraordinary sales when dream customers entered the store. I had a French tourist who tried every black one-piece bathing suit we had in the store in her size and purchased about 10 of them. She said that she needed them for her jacuzzi, which damaged bathing suits easily. I still don't know why she refused to buy other colors, considering that she was very thin and, therefore, didn't need a slimming color. She was from Southern Europe, where young women usually don't wear black one-piece bathing suits. It was an unbelievable sale that still intrigues me to this day. It was a lucky sale because the customer had come to shop during my shift. We rarely had two salespersons at the same time in the store.

Swim 'n Sport had no glitz, no designer to arrange the merchandise, no wowing dress code. The store had excellent lighting, but our sound system consisted of a small radio, with a missing antenna, that could play only one station audibly. It was quite a change from Swarovski, where Sandra had taught me that studies show how the volume of the radio has to be changed at different times of the day to stimulate customers. Peak times require a higher volume. At Swim 'n Sport, the music was kept fairly low, at all times. Salespersons were asked to wear skirts below their knees, to cover their shoulders, and to wear closed toe or peep-toe shoes. Colors didn't matter. The dress code was simple and in good taste. The company sent a secret shopper during one of my shifts. Thankfully, she rated my unpretentious skirt, blouse, and sandals as appropriate to sell beach clothing.

When I started working at Swim 'n Sport, I had no swimwear sales experience. However, having grown up with a pool, having been a very strong swimmer from an early age, and having spent my childhood vacations on beautiful beaches (as my parents strongly believed in the healing powers of the ocean), I always had a passion for swimwear that helped me assist the customers. I actually enjoyed picking store articles, from suits to hats.

I quickly learned that bathing suit purchases are culturally related and also stressful, emotional, and often connected to a woman's personal life. No matter the age, each customer had problems to solve: too small on top, too big on top, too wide on the hips, too wide on the stomach, too short or too tall. There was the difference between a bust that had been surgically built, which required no special support, and a naturally large bust which caused all sorts of problems. This means that two customers with exactly the same size required completely different bathing suits. Then, we had the customer with a scar to hide on her back; or the customer purchasing a suit to be worn at a children's party that allowed movement without being revealing; or the woman who was going to swim in the ocean and immediately afterwards to have lunch at an outdoor restaurant with the man she liked. She was looking for a one-piece suit and a long elegant sarong to cover her legs. Then, we had a customer who needed some nice-looking suits to wear in Hawaii, where the parents of her fiancé had invited her to spend a vacation in their beach house. To complicate matters, there were cultural constraints and beliefs, and often lack of self-esteem to account for. The multiple requests required the ability to solve physical problems and fulfill practical and cultural expectations. Once, I had a Brazilian young woman who was selecting a variety of bikini tops.

"Don't you need the bottoms also?" I asked her.

She looked at me with a disgusted expression.

"I don't do American bottoms!"

I laughed and understood because, as a woman with a Southern European cultural background, I didn't do American bottoms either, although I didn't wear Brazilian bottoms. They are cut differently. On the other hand, most American women generally liked American style bottoms.

I had a foreign customer, who came to the store with an American friend. She was visiting the United States and her friend insisted that she should buy a bathing suit, rather than bathe in the ocean with clothes on. The longest and most covering suits with a skirt that we had in the store seemed too risqué to this foreign customer. I had a similar situation later at Lord & Taylor, where a customer wanted to cover her legs as much as possible. These customers had impossible requests for bathing suit styles that don't exist. They both walked out without purchasing anything.

Salespersons were allowed to dress only specific floor mannequins. Managers had to prepare the wall displays, according to specific rules dictated by the company. Each month, the corporate office sent us a poster featuring a different bathing suit. The manager was responsible for placing that particular bathing suit plus two other ones of the same brand on the three mannequins in the store window. The poster was also placed in the store window. It was a very powerful ad because it always portrayed a stunning beach background and phenomenal bathing suits. Each mannequin could have only two articles, such as the suit and a bag or the suit and a hat, although we craved to add more. However, the focus had to be on the bathing suit. The front window display was a crucial marketing point. Tourists walked up and down Plaza Real, the Mizner Park main road, window shopping while eating an ice cream or relaxing after the beach. Most stores kept the store doors open. At Swim 'n Sport we were supposed to keep the front door closed, which discouraged customers. Occasionally, a customer peaked through the glass door, wondering if we were open. As I opened the door, the customer would say:

"I thought you were closed!"

After my first manager resigned, Gloria replaced her. She worked through the summer, meaning the worst time of the year for Swim 'n Sport. She was unhappy because the store didn't achieve its unrealistic goals.

One month, the corporate office sent us a poster featuring Longitude, a brand that makes one-piece bathing suits with a slightly longer torso for tall women. This brand can also fit some plus-size women, but it isn't meant for regularly sized women. The bathing suit on the model looked gorgeous and many women entered the store inquiring about it. However, it didn't fit most women because it was too long. It was really a specialty suit. In December, we had a poster with the Miraclesuit, which is a specialty suit for plus size women. Two mannequins wore black one-piece suits, and one mannequin wore a one-piece sparkling blue suit that was a special-order item, because we didn't carry it in the store. This didn't help our sales at all. Christmas is cruising time and celebration time. Many women inquired about the sparkling suit, but the two black suits were in no way suggesting a holiday time nor getting any attention.

At the end of the summer, the company decided to open a store in the Boca Raton Town Center Mall where traffic was good. Gloria was sent to manage the new store and was replaced by Denise. Our store was gradually going out of business. The corporate office had stopped restocking us. I had the impression that the company expected us to sell as much merchandise as possible before closing. Our Trina Turk collection (which was a big seller) was sent to the Town Center Mall. Customers entered our store asking for specific Trina Turk bathing suits.

"They have that suit at your other store in the mall! I thought I would save some time coming here!" a customer said, meaning that from then on, she was probably going to go directly to the other store.

Denise's first preoccupation was to purchase an electric espresso machine, as we had to spend entire shifts in the store alone, without the possibility of taking a break. On Sundays, I opened and closed the store, spending the entire day alone. If I needed to go to the bathroom, I had to rush. We weren't allowed to lock the front door. When a customer entered the store, the door made a chime alerting me of the visitor's presence. I had to rush out of the bathroom in the back of the store as quickly as I could. The keyholder of a shoe store told me that using the bathroom in a rush was a common occurrence in other Mizner Park stores.

Denise was upset because the company didn't want to pay for a special table on which to place her espresso machine.

"Did the espresso machine arrive?" she used to ask, entering the store. Her package arrived after a couple of weeks. My shift happened to partially overlap with her shift. She disappeared in the back of the store while I was assisting a customer in the fitting room. A few minutes later, she stormed to the front of the store, screaming:

"Is this red? Does this look red to you? Is it RED?!"

"No, it's not. How is the suit fitting?" I replied and continued to assist the customer, hoping that Denise would lower her voice.

She was angry and not ready to stop.

"It's NOT red! It's ORANGE! I ordered RED! This is ORANGE!"

Finally, she returned to the back of the store. When I went to the stockroom to retrieve an article, I found her on the phone yelling.

"Can I speak with your supervisor? Let me speak with your supervisor!"

She sent back the coffee maker and had to wait for another week to receive a second one. When she was finally able to brew coffee inside the store, she was unhappy with me because I refused to drink it. Working with her was stressful.

Working in retail requires constant adjustments to ever-changing work conditions. Managers and employees are constantly being replaced, personalities are different, expectations are high, and paychecks are on the line. Stores are never perfect. Some places are better than others. Customer service is a key component of the success of a store. Shoppers control us and depend on us at the same time. When in-store customer service is unsatisfactory, they shop online.

Lack of customer service can cause legal problems. Soon after I clocked in for an afternoon shift, an angry British man called. His wife was a loyal customer of our store. Each year, as the couple visited Boca Raton, she made her purchases in our store. After returning to England the previous summer, she discovered that one of the bathing suits she had purchased had a manufacturing defect. Therefore, on a business trip to the United States, her husband brought the suit back to exchange it or get a refund without a receipt. Audrey, another part-time employee, had taken pictures of the defect in the morning and sent them to Denise, asking her to call the British man as she had promised him. The man had waited for the manager's phone call, but she hadn't called him. She didn't want to talk to him because he had no receipt.

When I picked up the phone, the man told me that he was leaving for England in two days and if the matter wasn't resolved, he was going to have his lawyer contact the company. I gave him the number of the corporate office in Miami. Then, I notified the corporate office, explaining the situation. A couple of days later, the district manager contacted me and thanked me for alerting the corporate office. The matter had been resolved with a merchandise return without the intervention of a lawyer. Denise continued to harp for days that the customer shouldn't have received a refund without a receipt. All I could think of was that broken, dirty toilet brush that years earlier Linens 'n Things had replaced with no argument.

Denise expected me to break company rules. She used to place merchandise on hold for herself in the back of the store, for a long time. Since we weren't allowed to keep holds for longer than three days, she used fake names pretending that the holds were for somebody else. If a customer asked for one of her items on hold, I couldn't sell it.

"When are you planning to purchase these items?" I would ask her.

"When I get my next paycheck!"

When she got paid, she purchased a few items and left the other ones on hold for additional weeks. One morning, I received a request for transfer from the corporate office. The transfer included one of her articles on an indefinite hold. I processed the transfer which had to be done on the same day of the request, specifying that one of the items was a manager's hold. Denise got very upset with me. She wanted me to postpone the transfer, which was against the rules.

Things went from bad to worse. Denise got upset with me because one of my sales ended about ten minutes after closing time, which she could verify on the computer. After the customer left, I had to perform closing procedures and place merchandise back where it belonged, which could require an extra 20 to 30 minutes. Closing involved counting money, preparing the bank deposit, calculations, data entry, phone call to the district manager to leave a message with daily performance figures. Previous managers understood that if the closing employee had a late customer, that employee would have to stay longer to complete closing tasks. Possibly, the manager shortened the schedule on a different day in the future to balance the hours. That wasn't the case with Denise. She didn't want me to clock out at a later time than the one printed on the schedule. She didn't want late customers, which was unavoidable. If for any reason I was late, she asked me to close the register, clock out, and then put away the merchandise and prepare the store for the next day.

Asking an employee to work off the clock creates a risky situation. If an employee gets injured or if something happens inside the store later than clock-out time, the employee is in trouble because working off the clock is illegal. It was a particularly dangerous situation because I was alone in the store during closing time. If anything happened after I clocked out, I would have been liable.

I started pressuring late customers out of the store, preventing sales.

"I'm sorry, but the store is closing in ten minutes," I announced.

I also started leaving articles in the fitting rooms or on the counter when I had no time to put them away. My job was no longer sustainable in this store. In January 2013, I resigned. I set up an appointment with the district manager explaining to her why I was leaving. Audrey, my part-time coworker, resigned a week later. Shortly afterwards, the corporate office representatives appeared in the store and shut it down.

4

It's Hollywood! It's Hollywood!

Before resigning from Swim 'n Sport, I tried to get hired by one of the other retailers in Mizner Park, indicating to the managers that our store was probably going to close soon. We hadn't been properly restocked in three months. It was difficult to sell a bathing suit when one couldn't find a top that matched the bottom or vice versa. The leading brands had disappeared. No one was hiring. However, several managers mentioned that in the fall, Lord & Taylor was planning to reopen one of its stores in Florida, specifically in Mizner Park. They were looking forward to the reopening of Lord &Taylor, which was going to be an anchor store in Mizner Park. They told me to be ready to apply there.

It was January 2013. I needed a job immediately and couldn't wait until the fall. Therefore, I continued to look for employment. I was hired by the Natuzzi furniture store in Fort Lauderdale. Training lasted several days, without pay. Mr. Lorenzi, the store manager, was a very nice Italian man, who focused instruction on couches and chairs. At the end of my training, I knew all about different types of leather and ways to customize a sofa to match a customer's needs. However, the first person that I assisted

71

asked me about Natuzzi modular furniture pieces of which I knew nothing about. Several customers asked me about patio furniture, made by other companies. We sold patio furniture in our store because Natuzzi was linked to a South Florida distributor, which was the true company that had hired me. Mr. Lorenzi was under the impression that all customers were interested in Natuzzi leather sofas because that's what Natuzzi is known for around the world. He displayed a form of sacred reverence for the leather couches in the store and used to become impatient when my coworker Mercedes couldn't remember the types of leather to be used on specific sectionals. I drew a map of the store floor and memorized all the merchandise we had. Next, I tried to remember all there was to know about different leathers and different sofa styles. However, many customers continued to come in asking for patio umbrellas or wood furniture.

The sale of leather sofas took time. Usually, customers came in to inquire about styles and prices, but weren't ready to buy. They were probably checking multiple stores and making comparisons. Mercedes wasn't happy with the slow pace of the sales. She was planning to move to the Rooms To Go furniture store where, as she explained, traffic was much higher, sales were frequent, and customers made purchases quickly. She didn't care about the difference in quality between a luxury furniture store like Natuzzi and Rooms To Go. That's probably why she never bothered to properly memorize the types of leather we offered. I wasn't happy at Natuzzi either. On my last day of work, I watched Mercedes design a customized sectional sofa with incorrect sizes for a foreign customer. She was convinced that one foot equaled 26 inches. I interjected to correct her mistake, but Mercedes dismissed me quickly. She continued her mad calculations that led to a customized order with wrong sizes. I resigned the following day, running away from that job as fast as I could. I had been there for about a week.

In February 2013, Walgreens in Boca Raton hired me as a cashier on the main register. During my interview, Nick, the store manager, told me that entry level pay was $8/hour, but the company allowed growth based on performance. I was working over 35 hours a week. The store was very well managed. From the beginning, I clearly knew my duties and manager's expectations. Schedules were posted regularly. Working hours were predictable.

My job wasn't just a cashier job, but also required sales. Each day, before I started my shift, the manager on duty told me how many pieces of candy or batteries or bags of chips I was supposed to sell, or how many donations I was supposed to collect that day. I had to solicit my sales and I did exceed them significantly. My managers were happy with me and I probably had a good chance of moving up in the company, had I stayed long enough. Nick, the general manager, was on top of his store. One day, he ran out of his office to kick out a customer who used to come into the store to steal. Nick had seen him on camera from his office.

Walgreens collected donations for specific charities. Collecting these donations was important because our store was rated against other stores in the same district. Collecting donations was easy, as long as one presented the cause succinctly with effective wording that touched the customers' emotions. On one occasion, we were collecting for the Ronald McDonald House.

"What is the Ronald McDonald House?" I asked one of the managers so that I could prepare my sales pitch.

"It's a place where children can stay when they don't have a home" she replied in a hurry.

I understood that it was a house for homeless children. I assumed that the children were orphaned children. My pitch worked because even tourists who didn't speak English well, understood the word "orphans." I was collecting a lot of money for orphaned children.

"Keep the change for donations," said many customers, before leaving. Sometimes, the change amounted to $20-$30. Observing my success, a cashier who took over the main register after my shift ended, asked me what my method was.

"How do you get so many donations? I hardly get any," he said.

"I ask the customers if they want to donate for orphaned children. They all seem to be willing to help as soon as they hear the word *orphans*," I explained.

"Are the children orphans?" he asked.

"I'm not sure. A manager told me that the house is for children who are homeless."

My coworker also started mentioning the word *orphans* in his donation request and was very excited by the results. Word got around. Nick found out that we were collecting money for orphans and immediately clarified that the donations were for the construction of a Ronald McDonald House, where the children could live temporarily if, for example, they needed surgery far away from their home residence. They probably had a family. We had to stop using the word *orphans*. It didn't matter in the end because we had collected a large amount of donations for needy children. Nick was extremely happy with the collected donations, which bumped up our store position significantly in the district, as he told me. I had been identified as a successful salesperson at Walgreens because I was also moving sales of assigned products very fast.

Our store was located on a very important intersection of Boca Raton, surrounded by businesses, banks, and residences. I had an unending flow of customers during my shift. Most of them were repetitive customers who expected me to remember the type of cigarettes they smoked, without having to specify. That was challenging for me because I had never smoked in my life and knew nothing about cigarettes. Walgreens was a true neighborhood store. If you worked at Walgreens, you learned who had a husband in the hospital or a father in need of special care. You found out what health problem the customer was buying treatment for.

The entire staff was very friendly. Paul, one of my favorite managers, had a very positive attitude. I still remember him frequently uttering the word "Fantastic!" which used to resonate inside the store. One day, he noticed that I had some cough drops from CVS, our competitor. He never stopped getting on my case and joking about that. He finally confessed that he had a sister who worked as a manager at CVS. We all worked hard and had a good laugh.

Unfortunately, I developed severe allergies in that store. I had watery eyes and a runny nose. I was coughing and sneezing throughout my shift. The problem seemed to increase over time. After two months, I was constantly blowing my nose and eating cough drops. It was difficult to work that way. One day, after blowing my nose during my entire 7-hour shift, I went home and as I took a shower, my nose started bleeding heavily. I had never had a nose bleed before and that scared me.

The job required extreme accuracy as I was handling very large amounts of cash that had to be picked up by the managers multiple times during my shift. My register was counted before I started my shift, each time I left for my break, and at the end of my shift. I had to be fast and precise, but my in-store allergy made my job stressful. Although Walgreens was in many ways the right job for me, my health appeared to be jeopardized and my pay was low.

My position at Walgreens paid $8/hour, which was less than what I was previously earning in other stores when I resigned: $10.20/hour at Swarovski, $9.25/hour at Swim 'n Sport, $8.06/hour at Victoria's Secret, and $9.00/hour at Linens 'n Things. Swarovski paid well, but cut hours. My last bonus check at Swarovski was higher than my last paycheck. Walgreens seemed like the best job I had had at that point because it offered me the possibility to grow within the company, although the allergy during my shift was unbearable.

The fact that retail workers are trapped within low-income retail employment is not a coincidental occurrence. Trying to find employment with higher pay can be tricky because all retail jobs have a catch. There is always the risk of ending up in a worse situation. Yet, I moved on with my job search. In April 2013, I started the hiring process for a sales job at Wyndham Vacation Ownership, which was a sales job within the hospitality industry. This job required an online test and multiple interviews. The hiring process was long. As my Walgreens allergy required a quick resolution, I also applied for a job in a furniture store called World of Decor, which I had spotted in Deerfield Beach. I drove back to the store multiple times, asking the manager if he was interested in hiring me. On my third trip there, he looked at me and said:

"I'm going to hire you because you seem very persistent."

I resigned my position at Walgreens. Both Nick, the store manager, and Alicia, the assistant manager, tried to protect me. They asked me to work in their store only once a week, promoting and selling beauty products in the Beauty area. Alicia explained that if I resigned, it was going to be impossible for me to get rehired by Walgreens in the future. By keeping one day of work there, I could return with a full schedule, if needed. I turned down their offer because I didn't want to deal with my allergy in the store.

World of Decor sold mostly imitation antique furniture and also some modern furniture. It also sold fountains, entrance gates, large outdoor statues, lamps, ceiling medallions, and anything that could improve the appearance of a property.

Let us turn your house into an estate! said one of the signs posted inside the store.

As I quickly discovered, the store had very little traffic. While waiting for customers, Charles, a longtime salesman who looked to be in his 70s, used to sit at a 17th century style desk. John, a slightly younger looking salesman, sat on a Rococo looking armchair. I sat on one of the chairs surrounding a long table that seemed to have come out of a dining room in the Versailles palace. Charles listed our names on a sheet of paper. Each time we assisted a customer, we were supposed to put a checkmark next to our name. It was an unnecessary system considering that the store hardly had any traffic. We chatted, but our conversation came to an end when, occasionally, we saw a car pulling into the parking lot.

"Customer! Customer!" one of us announced like the men on Christopher Columbus' ship shouting "Land! Land!" We all got up and took position to see who was entering the store. Once, a couple walked in. As soon as he saw them, Charles whispered:

"They are holding hands! You know what that means, right?" I looked at him, uncomprehendingly.

"When they hold hands, they don't buy," he explained.

I didn't take his statement seriously. However, time after time, I had the opportunity to verify that couples entering a store holding hands usually never buy.

World of Decor allowed customers to negotiate prices, although no customer ever tried to do so. The store held auctions, which were very successful. Only during an auction, a large crowd filled the store.

Checking and retrieving an item from another location was problematic. The stockroom was messy. I had a customer who asked to buy a five-piece bedroom set including the 12-piece comforter set on display. The comforter set couldn't be found in the stockroom, although we had it. The displayed set couldn't be sold. Therefore, I lost part of the sale. Ten days after I started my job, we were told that World of Decor was going to close our location.

Thankfully, I was hired almost immediately within the hospitality industry by Wyndham Vacation Ownership in Pompano Beach. My new timeshare sales job promised very high pay, and indeed I started having sales immediately. However, about a month after I started my job, suddenly most potential buyers sent to the resort were unable to pass a credit check. All salespersons were having the same problem. The potential customers went on their tours, expressed their interest in purchasing timeshare points, but couldn't get a loan. Sometimes, both husband and wife didn't pass the credit check. My pay dropped. Without commission, I was earning only base pay, which was the minimum wage of $7.79/hour.

Transportation logistics were also complicated. My daughter had a summer job as the assistant of a real estate agent. We had one car. We drove to Pompano Beach very early in the morning. Twice a week, before starting work at the resort where the sales office was located, I had training in a different location. Therefore, my daughter waited for me and then we drove to the Wyndham resort, where I worked for the rest of the day. My daughter drove back to Boca Raton to start her day of work. After my work day ended, I waited a couple of hours for my daughter to pick me up. Then we drove back to Boca Raton. It was difficult although another salesperson told me that she drove from Miami to Pompano Beach every day.

I left Wyndham during my six-week sales training period that followed the initial classroom instruction. There was no time to be wasted if customers were unable to buy. I will always highly respect Wyndham because this company gave me exceptional training that was going to help me in all my subsequent sales jobs. Timeshare vacations worked well for many people. Wyndham constantly added resorts to its already wide selection, allowing travelers to book their vacations with ease. Wyndham timeshare owners frequently came in to purchase more points.

While I was employed at Wyndham, I heard that there were other timeshare companies that used lies to close a sale. We never had to do that. We always told our clients what their timeshare purchase consisted of. Nothing was concealed. We sold timeshares for beautiful resort locations and made many families happy. One of my coworkers, who had previously worked for another hospitality company in Orlando, told us the story of an employee who had amazing sales. Everyone was curious to learn his successful method. This employee told his clients that Shamu, the whale, was channeled from Disney territory into a small lake in front of the timeshare resort, to practice for its shows. They believed him. His sales came to an end when his company found out and fired him. It was a humorous episode for Wyndham salespersons because we presented the facts and our clients clearly knew what they were purchasing.

One day, I walked into Walgreens. Both Nick and Alicia came out to greet me. They asked me if I was making money. I replied that I wasn't because our clients suddenly didn't seem to pass their credit checks.

"I told you! You should have kept a foot in the door when you left," said Alicia.

"We can't rehire you," explained Nick. They were sad because they would have been happy to take me back. I didn't regret my decision to leave. It was better that Walgreens couldn't rehire me because the in-store allergy would have made me feel miserable.

After leaving Wyndham, I was interviewed for a sales position at the Baer's Furniture store in Boca Raton. My interviewer was willing to hire me. He said he was saving a spot for me in the required classroom training, which started in September. It was an honor because Baer's Furniture was a highly successful store and could only take a limited number of salespersons.

"Can you promise me that you won't apply for any other job before September?" he asked me.

I didn't expect this question and I froze because it was the end of July and I needed an income until September. I let the panic show on my face without voicing my concern. I should have asked whether I was allowed to take a temporary job until September. Instead, I remained silent, while a whirlwind of thoughts spiraled in my mind.

"I understand," he said, without understanding anything at all. "I'm sorry, but I won't be able to add you to our classroom training in September," he continued, getting up and dismissing me from the interview.

How could my interviewer expect applicants to accept a job that starts two months later, without allowing them the possibility to earn money to pay their bills until the starting date? I left the interview feeling disappointed and perplexed by his question, although I should have clearly expressed my monetary concern.

Perhaps the store was aware of the upcoming Lord & Taylor interviews and was afraid of losing applicants.

In August 2013, Lord & Taylor started interviewing for positions in the new store that was about to open in Mizner Park. It was going to be one of its "Jewels," meaning a store that wasn't inside a shopping center. My first interviewer offered me a commission job in the Jewelry department. I rejected this option as I was afraid of the low traffic in Mizner Park. After reviewing my past experience, he hired me as a part-time salesperson in Ladies Swimwear, Lingerie, and Accessories. During my second interview, my future manager decided that my pay was going to be $9.50/hour, which the Human Resources representative later bumped up to $9.75/hour. It was a good entry pay and I liked my future manager. She was a very nice and experienced ex-employee of Nordstrom. Unfortunately, on my first day of work, I found out that she had been assigned to a different area of the store. Time after time, I could never keep my hiring manager as my manager. I always ended up with a different person.

Working for a new store is a very interesting experience. When I first entered our building, I saw bare walls, empty racks, and empty tables. A month later, it was a spectacle of luxurious displays. A very pleasant perfume scent welcomed anyone entering the store. The stereo sound system was outstanding. The lighting was amazing. Fashion ruled majestically. We were trained in August. Then, we helped stock the store, which opened to the public in

October. During the stocking period, we were allowed to wear jeans and sandals. We had a schedule that was going to remain limited until the store officially opened.

In order to increase my income, I started looking for a second job. A second job can't be in competition with a first job. This means that I couldn't work for a company that sold the same type of merchandise sold by Lord & Taylor. I couldn't sell clothes, shoes, jewelry, cosmetics, accessories, or lingerie. One of my coworkers told me that she was working at Walgreens once a week, although Walgreens sold cosmetics. Out of desperation, I tried to get hired at Walmart, which sold cosmetics as well as clothing, shoes, accessories, and lingerie.

The Walmart manager who interviewed me was willing to hire me and didn't care about the fact that I was working at Lord & Taylor. However, an obstacle made this match impossible. The Walmart schedule was generated every three weeks. The Lord & Taylor schedule was posted once a month, after the Walmart schedule had already been posted. I continued my search with determination. Having multiple jobs in my resume never worked against me. I usually listed only the jobs relevant for the position I was seeking and discarded the other ones. It was like pulling rabbits out of my hat and utilizing them as needed. As I kept moving from one business to another, I was gaining experience in different areas and becoming very "marketable."

I was hired by Subway with a pay of $8/hour. After a week of employment, Ryan, the store manager, asked me if I wanted to work at Subway full-time for $9.00/hour. I thought it was a strange offer. He didn't even know how I was going to perform and he was willing to increase my pay and status within a week. I stressed the fact that my job at Subway was my second job because my employment at Lord & Taylor paid me more. I think pay was the only factor he was able to understand.

I wasn't comfortable at Subway. Money in the tills was counted in a rush and often incorrectly. My cashier job also included some dishwashing. We used tap water that contained soap and disinfectants. Since I felt a burning sensation in my eyes, I started wearing glasses instead of contact lenses during my shifts. Tanya, who was also a server, showed me how to clean the bathrooms, without using gloves. She told me she had allergies and rashes on her hands, but she didn't want to use gloves when handling chemicals. I bought a pair of thick plastic gloves at the grocery store to use when I washed dishes. Under my thick pair, I wore two layers of light plastic gloves supplied by Subway, to prevent moisture from getting inside. I also used several layers of gloves when I cleaned the bathrooms. Robert, another server, told me that he had been fired by Subway for not washing his hands before wearing gloves, as required. However, the company had rehired him. I worked at Subway from August 2014 to the end of September 2014 and resigned without notice. My eye inflammation was resolved after I stopped working there. Lord & Taylor was about to open to the public and I was finally going to get 20-25 hours of work each week.

Lord & Taylor had very knowledgeable and experienced designers who controlled all aspects of its displays: position of fixtures, colors, mannequins, hanging of signs on the walls, ways to place products on the tables. Like most of the managers, the designers had been sent from New York to work in our store. They were driven by aesthetics, checking from a distance the flow of lines, colors, and shapes. Like one of my coworkers at the Hilton Grand Vacations used to say, "It's Hollywood! It's Hollywood!"

I still have immense respect for these designers, although I was constantly frustrated with them during my work. For example, they liked to place hangers on the display racks with the hooks turned to the right side. They claimed that a series of hooks facing that direction positively contributed to the overall visual result. It was awkward for a right-handed person like me to hold a hanger with the hook pointing in the right direction and even the customers often commented about it.

When a salesperson placed an item incorrectly on a table, the head designer would appear out of nowhere almost instantly.

"If you don't put the clothes back the way they were displayed, I will report you!" was his terrifying threat.

I looked up to him, but I was also scared of him. Clothes had to be folded properly and piled up in size order. How did this head designer appear so fast to catch something out of order? If we sold the last hat on a mannequin and replaced it with a new hat (as no one would dare leave the mannequin's head uncovered), the designers quickly replaced it. They always noticed and changed what we chose. We weren't allowed to remove clothes from a mannequin if it had to be taken apart. This is a common practice in most stores because mannequins are very expensive. In the middle of a sale, I had to call a designer to take a bathing suit off a mannequin. Designers weren't in the store on Saturday and Sunday, which means that on those days we couldn't sell clothes on the mannequins. Once, on a Sunday, I called the manager because a customer had asked for an activewear shirt that was on a mannequin. Activewear was part of my area, Lingerie. The manager refused to take the mannequin apart to remove the shirt, which wasn't available online. I think everyone was afraid of designers! Yet, I am aware of the crucial importance of their role in a store. They are the silent heroes of any major store. They make decisions that affect the visual impact of the store on customers. A store with poor design isn't inviting. Disorderly layout indicates greater problems below the surface and store dysfunction.

My manager asked me to hide all the tags inside the bathing suits. This irritated customers who looked at me and barked:

"Why do you hide all the tags? One can't see sizes!"

They pulled all the tags out of the suits until they found their size. Then, as they picked up the hangers, they stared at the hooks with a puzzled expression. We just continued to hide the tags and turn the hangers as required. Ultimately, we wanted to have a perfect looking store.

The festivities for the opening of the store lasted a week. The mayor participated in the ribbon cutting ceremony. Numerous TV stations were present. On the night of our soft opening, the store generously catered champagne and food for the guests. They weren't true buying customers, but rather browsers, to whom a handful of employees, including myself, opened credit card accounts. Solid sales began the following day.

The Lord & Taylor dress code was strict, although it allowed some flexibility. We could choose colors and styles as long as we wore jackets, and as long as our shoes had a strap in the back and were closed toe or peep-toe. Women could choose to wear slacks or skirts or dresses. Men wore suits.

Joselyn, the store general manager, was an exceptional administrator, capable of intelligent marketing to draw customers into the store. She supervised all aspects of the store, from employee training to customer relations. She was present during our job interviews and was always very accessible to all of us. Joselyn attended luncheons and meetings with important professional and social associations of Palm Beach County, advertising the store, extending invitations, and organizing events. During my eight-month employment period, the store held charity events, Friends and Family events, a Prom event for mothers and daughters, parties with a DJ and food samples from the main restaurants in our area. We even had a high school marching band moving around the store once. I never got bored at this store. It was really fun to work there.

Since weekday mornings were slow, Joselyn distributed special coupons during the first two hours after opening. The store also distributed promotional gifts. Customers who opened a credit card account received an umbrella with the Lord & Taylor logo. Customers loved these umbrellas, which were beautiful and useful in Florida. Merchandisers also brought gifts. During an event, I had the honor of being assisted by three merchandisers in the swimwear area. Two of them represented two major bathing suit brands and one represented the popular Havaianas flip flops. They brought their expertise and gifts to the customers, staying for most of the day.

Upon hiring, I was told that with good performance, I could have been promoted to a full-time position. I worked very hard to keep my sales high. I was truly captivated by Lord & Taylor since the first day I set foot in the store. I swore to myself that I was going to be a manager one day. Lord & Taylor is the only store where I truly desired and planned to become a manager. I strived to achieve my goal. Month after month, I was among the top five salespersons of the store for sales volume. In March 2015, Joselyn invited me and four other employees to an award luncheon in a Mizner Park restaurant, for opening the largest number of credit card accounts.

It was a formal acknowledgment of performance. I also became part of the President's Club, a prestigious sales award that allowed me to wear a special badge and to have special business cards that indicated my status to the customers. As Joselyn explained, when customers saw the President's Club badge, they recognized an experienced and successful employee. The badge encouraged their trust and indirectly led to sales.

Receiving credit for one's good work makes an employee feel appreciated and accepted by management. I believe that management's acknowledgment of good work is one of the factors that promotes retainment, especially when combined with the possibility of advancement. However, monitoring sales publicly creates friction among the staff members because less successful employees feel ignored. Managers used to post the names of the top 5 performers of the previous day on a daily sheet that everyone read in the break room. It was problematic for high achievers. Monthly recognition was also posted on a huge board in the break room. The board listed names and figures. Monthly recognition included a short ceremony, in which all managers read the names of their top producers and made some positive comments. This ceremony included free breakfast and was usually attended only by the employees nominated for the month. The other employees felt completely excluded. The managers also posted a sheet that listed the names of non-performers, who were encouraged to start performing.

This system reminded me of Wyndham posting the salespersons' names and volume of sales on a blackboard. One of the managers cautioned me not to talk to salespersons who had low sales. The blackboard was supposed to determine our social interaction because the managers believed that salespeople with low sales brought down morale. He was partly correct as unsuccessful salespersons made negative comments. However, we all socialized, regardless of the managers' recommendations. We shared details about our sales and tips for success. We learned from one another.

At Lord & Taylor, I had no friends within my area. My friends were in other departments. My coworker Bella once interrupted one of my sales in Accessories.

"Let me continue. You probably already made enough money for today!" she said in front of the customer.

Was I supposed to stop selling for the day? Why didn't these employees have their own customers? Customers were free roaming people that anyone could have approached. My sly coworkers waited for me to establish rapport and prepare the customer for the sale. Then, they interrupted.

One of my friends in the Shoe department recommended that I give away some of my sales to low producers. I took his advice on a very small scale. I was trying to keep my performance high to be promoted to full-time status and, eventually, to a managerial position. I gave a few sales to Bella because I felt sorry for her, but it wasn't dignifying for the store to have employees walking around taking over sales. Moreover, customers don't like to be shifted to a different salesperson after handing a few articles to be rung up to the first salesperson.

My articles on hold were always sold by somebody else without my number, although I always used my coworkers' numbers to sell their articles on hold. My manager, Valery, used to say that it didn't matter because we weren't on commission. She thought that we were completely interchangeable, although our sales were monitored on a daily basis. I had a friend in the Dresses department, where occasionally they would send me to cover a lunch or an absence. She was the only employee who ever rang up one of my holds with my number. Sales in Dresses could take over an hour. Therefore, employees in that area got organized and started working together. They were tired of working for hours without getting credit. They always rang up holds with the correct number and if a salesperson had to leave in the middle of a sale, they gave credit for the sales placed by the person that was leaving.

One day, while I was in the middle of a long sale, Valery called me to remind me that I was supposed to clock out soon, as my shift was ending. The customer had already picked three bathing suits and was still trying various styles. She was a shy middle-aged woman.

"You know, this is very difficult for me..." she explained when she first arrived. "I haven't bought a bathing suit in many years, neglecting myself. I need to buy some suits, but my body is no longer what it used to be..."

I understood. I had been exposed to so many problems at Swim 'n Sport that I knew how miserable she must have been feeling. She had aged and gained weight, and if I had to make a guess, she probably had gotten divorced and was trying to pick herself up in bits and pieces. She really needed help. With a lot of patience, I checked outside of the fitting room how each bathing suit and brand fit on her. Miracle Suit was a good choice. I went into the stockroom and looked for styles and colors that weren't on the sales floor in her size. She patiently tried on every suit I handed to her and started making her choices. Valery's call left me in a difficult predicament.

"I'm so sorry. That was my manager on the phone. I have to clock out soon. Would you like me to place these suits on hold and continue another day? Or do you prefer to continue with another salesperson?" I asked her. She was dismayed.

"You have been helping me for an hour. If you don't ring me up, I won't buy anything!" she said.

This customer felt abandoned after she had placed her trust in me. I told her I was going to clock out and come back. I just couldn't abandon her while she was trying on a bathing suit. I clocked out, came back, and continued to help her against the rules. I had to rush a little and she knew it. She added a fourth bathing suit, but the sale wasn't completed properly. I didn't have time to discuss cover-ups or other items that would have increased the price of my sale. I led the woman to the Men's department, which was next to Swimwear, where my friend Brandon was working. I asked him to ring up the bathing suits with my number explaining that I had clocked out, but the customer wanted me to get credit for her purchases. The woman backed me up, repeating that she wasn't going to buy anything unless I got credit. I was very happy to see her leave satisfied, although I felt like an outlaw for completing the sale after clocking out. Later, I returned the favor. If customers asked me for help in the Men's department, I would take them straight to Brandon. Lord & Taylor wasn't a perfect store, but overall, it was one of the best stores I worked for.

Valery didn't seem to care about my performance and seemed oblivious to some of the problems that prevented a boosting of sales in Swimwear. I told her that we needed more bikinis and more active swimwear.

"All swimwear customers are fat and old," she said. "We don't need more bikinis and active swimwear."

I constantly had requests for bikinis and swimsuits to be used for water sports. Valery was probably not in the least interested in swimming and water sports. She thought we could go on selling primarily Miracle Suits and one-piece bathing suits.

In January 2014, I was very disappointed to see a seasonal employee with lower sales than mine turn into a full-time employee, after 3 weeks of work. I started questioning whether I had placed my stakes on the wrong store. Was this company going to allow me to grow within its structure?

My working hours were insufficient, but I still had no intention of leaving my job, which I truly loved. Instead, I tried to add hours elsewhere. I inquired in restaurants, delis, ice cream shops, car dealerships, and any place that was compatible with my current job. One morning, I walked into a Middle-Eastern delicatessen store that had a long line of trays filled with cooked foods. There were no customers inside the store. I told the owner that I was working at Lord & Taylor and I was looking for a second job.

"Why? Why do you want to work so hard?" he asked me with sincere concern.

"I need more hours and more income," I replied.

"It's too much work! You don't need to work so hard!" he insisted. It was humorous. I left wondering if he made any money himself. Was anyone going to buy all that food he had prepared?

I applied for a sales job in a Chevrolet dealership, where I had already tried months earlier. I was interviewed by the same person.

"I liked you the first time," he said. Then, he added that if I really wanted the job, he was ready to hire me, but it would have been to my detriment because sales were very low and even the most productive salespersons in the dealership weren't doing well.

After multiple attempts, in February 2014, I was finally hired by Italio, a casual Italian restaurant where customers could build their meal from a variety of options. It was a very lucky second job. I had no allergies in this restaurant. The restaurant hired many college students and for this reason it produced its schedule weekly, based on student availability. On Thursday, the restaurant posted its schedule for the following week. I had a schedule for the entire month already posted by Lord & Taylor. The managers scheduled me on my days off. Mark, the general manager, offered me $8.50/hour, which was a very good entry pay. I worked 7-hour shifts two or three times a week, increasing my monthly income, after taxes, by about $400-$600 a month. I was now working seven days a week.

Mark was a very sharp manager. He paid attention to every detail and caught any discrepancy immediately. Once, I replenished the San Pellegrino beverage cans by taking a pack from the wrong side of the stockroom. He walked into the restaurant, immediately caught my mistake, and then showed me what to do. He was a good leader and everyone liked him. The restaurant had a very harmonious atmosphere with cooks, servers, dishwashers, and cashiers working well together. Work was very hard in this place. Besides cashiering, I had to set up the tables, chairs, and umbrellas outside, moving two heavy umbrella bases. Shortly after I started working there, someone stole one of the umbrellas, during a storm. This made my job so much easier in the morning! Now I only had to move one heavy umbrella base out of the store. I also had to carry heavy bags of trash outside and throw them into the bin. I stepped on top of a crate and managed to swing the bag up in the air and then down into the bin. Other duties included cleaning the windows and counters, sweeping the floors, replenishing the dining area, refilling sauces, bagging cookies, and cutting lemons, which were all very easy chores. I was unable to carry the enormous and heavy container of iced tea from the kitchen to the dining area. However, one of the cooks usually did it for me.

During peak time, I never left the register. I never took breaks in this job. Restaurants never give you set breaks. One takes a short break only if needed. Since I was responsible for the register count at the end of my shift, I avoided taking breaks. I didn't want to be responsible for a shared register. At the end of my 7-hour shift, I could eat a free meal, which was a good meal with shrimp or meat and vegetables. Free meals had to be eaten inside the store and couldn't be taken home.

The restaurant operations were very well orchestrated by all team members. We all worked non-stop, quickly communicating tasks or needs to each other. Servers and cashiers turned toward the cooks, naming the dishes that required extemporaneous cooking:

"Two fried calamari, three pesto breadsticks, one pepperoni..."

I handed the online orders printed by the register to the servers at the beginning of the serving line. The servers asked me for the dipping sauces in the refrigerator, near the cash register. The cooks alerted me when the requested dishes were ready. A manager was on the serving line calling the ingredients for which I had to charge extra, when the dish reached the register. It was a fast job that required constant multi-tasking, which wouldn't have been possible without good teamwork. We depended on each other.

Two young managers had been against hiring me due to my age, which was over 60. Mark, the general manager, and Pablo, the assistant manager, supported me. Pablo was in his 50s and had a good sense of humor.

"These young people look at me and think I am decrepit. They think I am already buried in the backyard! I'm not old! I like to go out dancing!" he used to tell me.

Mark, Pablo, and one of the two young managers (the other one had resigned) quickly realized that I wasn't decrepit either. They didn't know that I had a very athletic past, which included some serious swimming starting at a very young age. During my initial weeks of employment, Mark observed me, while I worked, to establish if I was right for the job. I would go outside carrying a large and heavy trash bag to be thrown into the bin, and as I turned, I would find him standing behind me, smiling. He observed everything and for that reason, he was an excellent restaurant manager.

During my first week of work, I didn't catch that one of the credit card payments hadn't gone through. If a payment wasn't processed successfully, the register printed a different type of receipt, a shorter one. Then, it would show a message on the screen indicating the missing payment, which I also didn't recognize. Tara, another cashier who was helping with my training, found the customer sitting at a table and asked him to use a different type of payment. The second time, the register printed a short receipt, I caught it. Mark, who always knew everything that happened, even if he was in a different part of the store, was extremely pleased. As soon as I became proficient, he asked me if I wanted to add hours during the days in which I worked at Lord & Taylor, but I really couldn't do it. For the first time in years of retail, everything was going well for me financially and logistically.

Mark came up with an incentive to increase employee motivation and improve task performance. He divided all employees into teams that were supposed to compete against each other. The winning team was going to go out for dinner with the manager leading that team. Mark was planning to pay for the dinner out of his own pocket. Every day, at the end of each shift, the manager on duty checked how tasks had been performed and graded the employees. If something hadn't been completed well, the employee had to correct it. Potentially, this contest could have caused friction, but no one took it very seriously because everyone seemed to know its outcome.

"Our team is going to win because Mark is our team leader and he never likes to lose," said Tara, who was on my team.

Convinced that I had a dinner party coming up, I started looking for a dress that was appropriate. At the end of my work shifts, I continued to stand for hours in clothing stores, looking for a graduation dress to wear at my daughter's upcoming college graduation and for the Italio dinner dress.

I had a busy life working seven days a week. In some ways, I felt like I had a double life: three to four times a week, I wore very dressy clothes at Lord & Taylor; two to three times a week, I wore jeans, a t-shirt with the Italio logo, and restaurant shoes. They were very clashing costumes. It was Hollywood at both stores!

5

Do You Like Your Customers?

If you don't like your customers, don't bother applying. Retail requires a passion for customer service. In spite of low wages and many other problems, retail workers usually like their customers, the nice ones and the difficult ones. They are constantly challenged by their customers seeking help. The grumpy ones who verbally attack the salesperson are usually the ones that need the most help. They don't have anything personal against the salesperson. They may be distressed by a problem they are trying to solve or they may be angry at the company that the salesperson represents.

Salespersons who go out of their way to assist an upset customer, with calm demeanor, can become the customer's favorite retail assistants. These retail workers prove to be professional by solving a problem and leaving the customer satisfied. They are dependable and trustworthy, allowing the customer to rely on them for future purchases. On the other hand, a salesperson who is troubled by a customer's behavior is an employee who allows his personal feelings to interfere with his business role. Yes, it's Hollywood all the time and assisting all customers, including grumpy ones, is part of the employee's role.

Customers aren't supposed to be perfect, friendly, or polite. They form a heterogeneous crowd that impacts a salesperson's paycheck. Good salespersons play their role well because they have an innate desire to please their customers and leave them satisfied. They truly believe in their customer service purpose on the sales floor. A complaint is always good because it's emotional and all sales are emotional. Complaining customers are always potential buyers. They'll express disappointment or dissatisfaction before considering a purchase option. If the salesperson listens to the complaint with genuine interest, the customer is likely to listen to the employee's suggestions. Complaints allow salespersons to find solutions and sell.

Some customers are annoying and extremely difficult, but they're always right. A difficult customer may want to test all options before making a choice. This customer may exhaust all possibilities in a variety of stores, including the online stores. Sales have to be placed at a fast pace, before the customer leaves the store because that customer may never come back. A customer buys from the store and from the salesperson. If you fall in love with a product, but you don't like your salesperson who didn't assist you properly, you won't buy in that store and you'll look for the same product elsewhere. That's how important customer service is and that's how important salespersons are for a business.

The way customers shop has gradually been changing over the past 20 years. Online retail is open 24 hours a day, all year, and doesn't require a trip to any store. The merchandise selection and price range are often wider online. Customers are no longer shopping in the stores as much as they used to. Low traffic is a generalized problem. As brick-and-mortar store profits are lost to the online stores, retailers adopt a variety of systems to attract customers. Some stores lower their prices, which isn't the best solution if the store is already struggling to stay afloat. It's the method used to sell during liquidations. When I first started working at World of Decor, most products were 50% off and some of them, like lamps, had a "buy one, get one free" promotion. I asked the manager if the store was closing, but he assured me that he was just running a limited yearly sale. The sale never ended while I worked at this store. Price cuts didn't seem to increase traffic. Discounts can be good, but not in a store that is already selling with difficulty.

Occasional and unlikely discounts outside of typical sale times, in a very successful store, will attract customers and increase sales. This happened once by error at Neiman Marcus. On a Monday afternoon, James, who was responsible for stocking and pricing, walked into Gift Gallery, equipped with price tags and signs.

"Some Mackenzie Childs prices changed," he announced.

"Did they go up a lot?" I asked.

"They actually...went down," he said, scrutinizing his paperwork.

Mackenzie Childs enamelware products never went down in price. Only some patterns went on sale one month a year. I interrupted everything I was doing, to pay attention and be ready to take pictures to send to my customers. James continued to announce that multiple pieces in various collections were 20% off.

"Courtly check also," he added after reading his list.

The courtly check collection never went on sale. I took pictures of the sale signs and products on the sale shelves and immediately started texting Mackenzie Childs customers with my company phone. Within a few seconds, in-state and out-of-state customers started placing orders. Some local customers asked me to place holds as they preferred to come into the store to select their pieces, since courtly check products have slight variations in color and design. The customers who came into the store added even more products to their selection, once they were in front of the sale shelves. By Wednesday, I had sold all the kitchen canisters and other very popular products in the Orlando store and in the warehouse. I started calling other stores to place a hold on their pieces, as I was ringing them up in my store. The employees in other stores had to attach an "option 7" tag on their products, which were going to be shipped directly from their locations to my customers.

"I am looking for some Mackenzie Childs pieces on sale," I would tell the employee who answered my call.

"We don't have any Mackenzie Childs pieces on sale."

"They are on sale in our store! 20% off!" The other store employees were in disbelief.

"Anyway, these are the pieces I need to ring up," I would cut the conversation short, so that the other employee could pull the products I needed quickly.

On Thursday, my manager discovered that the sale had been announced incorrectly. The sale signs were immediately removed and the remaining unsold pieces were placed back within their regularly priced collections. I was allowed to sell the pieces already on hold with the 20% discount. The customers who showed up during the weekend without holds couldn't get the discounted price. James and I laughed about that Mackenzie Childs sale for years afterwards. It was one of the most lucrative Mackenzie Childs events for me.

To attract customers, some stores allow them to download promotional offers to be used inside the store. At Lord & Taylor, coupons were easily available through electronic mail to all customers. Our manager discouraged us from reminding customers about these coupons unless it was crucial to close a sale. For example, if a customer didn't seem ready to buy, I discounted a $160 pair of designer sunglasses with an instant coupon that the customer could receive by texting a particular word to a particular number. I had to guide the customers who were totally unaware of this instant coupon. Right afterwards, if a second customer arrived and was willing to purchase a $350 pair of sunglasses without hesitation, I didn't mention the instant coupon. The store didn't want to cut its costs too much and I didn't want to lower my sales numbers.

Once inside the store, shoppers make unplanned, impulsive purchases. They also make larger purchases than they would online, if the salesperson upsells. However, there are factors that can reduce sales inside a store. At World of Decor, there were no barcodes to be scanned. If a price tag was missing on an item, a price search was required. In this store, a computer price search required the identification of a product on one screen and the actual price on another screen. If the item wasn't present in the first screen, we had to call the manager who could give us a price.

"Don't worry about it!" customers would say in the middle of a price search. When customers ask for a price, they expect a prompt answer.

World of Decor also had an inventory retrieval problem. For example, the store needed a couple of days to locate in the stockroom the 12-piece comforter set that I couldn't sell. The inability to match a fast online fulfillment center causes the store to lose its competitiveness.

Most stores tend to capture customers' information to remember their interests and offer personalized service. Salespersons often notate details about their customers' life: names of their family members and pets, birthday of a child, special family celebrations, professions, and anything that can lead to a sale in the future. At Neiman Marcus, I had multiple customers with dogs that I would contact whenever the appropriate products arrived in the store or in the system. One customer in particular had a little dog that lived like a king. He had multiple beds and couches and a bowl holder with a beautiful crown on top. I used to contact this customer when we received Christmas ornaments that looked like her dog, which she always purchased. She also bought from me a magnificent poster pet bed to be placed in a different room.

I wrote down the names of customers who collected particular crystal pieces, porcelain dishes, or Christmas ornaments. An elderly lady used to purchase one or two Anna Weatherley porcelain plates for her daughter each time I alerted her that they had a discount. As soon as the annual Strongwater "Twelve Days of Christmas" pieces or the annual Lalique ornaments became available, I contacted my collectors. These were quick sales that only required communicating with the customers, whose names were on my list.

I sold a child's car to a pregnant mother. The car was parked in the nursery for a long time. This mother was ready to purchase other products for her newborn child. I sold children's snorkeling products and candies with interesting shapes to a teacher, who constantly acquired items to give to her students. I sold a huge Santa's mailbox to a business owner who placed it in her main office. This lady also had two young daughters for whom she purchased multiple YSL handbags. I sold numerous Mark Roberts bunnies and eggs to a customer who organized lavish Easter parties for her large family. I sold very unusual Vista Alegre crystal decanters to a customer who collected decanters and loved showing them off to his friends. I sold original Chanel custom earrings with the Chanel logo to a customer who had a passion for the Chanel brand. I believe they had been worn by the models in a fashion show. The manager of the Jewelry department sent an email to all salespersons in the store.

"I have two authentic pairs of Chanel earrings. Let me know if your customers are interested."

I texted my customer in Fort Myers. She immediately responded, but she only bought one pair because the other pair had clips instead of posts.

If you had the right customer for the right product, the sale took place within a few seconds. The more detailed information one kept about a customer's life, the more one could sell. The wider and more diverse was the list of customers one developed through years of customer service, the higher the number of sales. Many of my customers lived in other cities or states, but I constantly texted images and information on products that I knew they would be interested in. Had I not sent this information to them, they would have never looked for these products online. The phone is a very powerful sales tool at Neiman Marcus.

Grocery stores, such as Fresh Market and Publix, attract customers advertising BOGO deals and weekly discounts on their app. Customers can sit comfortably on their couch, checking the list of promotions and planning their shopping list. Publix also offers coupons that can be printed at home or found in the store. It's a method of grocery shopping that utilizes tech tools for in-store or online shopping. This is the new way of shopping of our time, in which everything comes together. Online shopping and in-store shopping are no longer in opposition with each other. Customers check online availability and prices before making a purchase in a brick-and-mortar store. Online shoppers check availability and prices in physical stores. Tech tools are used to search, compare, and decide.

What can a store offer over online retail, besides better prices or immediate availability? Expertise, such as the ability of a cosmetics representative to match the right product and color to the skin. And, as my hiring manager at Neiman Marcus used to say:

"Customers shop in the store for the service that we offer to them."

Services are the trump card of brick-and-mortar stores. A personal shopper who helps a customer make a selection throughout the store offers a service that justifies a trip to the store. Today, personal shoppers can guide the customer throughout the store using FaceTime. After making their basic selection, customers go to the store to try the clothes on and possibly add some more. Some customers don't go to the store at all. They have their purchases shipped to them by the salesperson and return what they don't like. You can just imagine how the price of a purchase can rise, when driven by a trained personal shopper. Customers walked into Swarovski asking for bride's jewelry, birthday gifts, anniversary gifts, first communion gifts, gifts for the bridesmaids and more. Brides tried different combinations of necklaces, earrings, and bracelets offered by the salespersons. Although a virtual try-on jewelry experience offers many advantages, a real try-on experience assisted by a trained salesperson may deliver higher sales.

Some customers want to physically inspect and touch the products they are going to buy. Online reviews aren't always sufficient. Brick-and-mortar stores aren't easily replaceable when they offer services. Would you buy a couch without sitting on it, especially considering that, in most cases, you have to pay for the return of an online couch if you don't find it comfortable? Would you buy a car without test driving it? Would you buy house decor items without checking their color and texture next to samples of fabrics or tiles? Would you buy a scented candle without smelling it? What about shoes, clothes, or gowns that may require alterations? There are some customers willing to take a chance online. And yet, some Neiman Marcus customers drove two or three hours from their house to the store just to see, touch and compare the products they were interested in. These products were shown online, but many customers preferred to purchase them in the store.

Swimwear is a difficult category that requires a trip to the store unless one wants to purchase a bathing suit in a brand and style that one is already familiar with. The selection of a bathing suit often requires the resolution of problems. Therefore, a trip to the store is always more effective than an online search. Customers are more willing to go to the physical store when they have a regular salesperson that they trust.

It's difficult to predict whether shopping will become completely automated. For now, it's a complex process that keeps the physical aspect alive and utilizes more and more sophisticated technological tools. As in-store shopping requires more advanced systems to attract customers and take them away from the convenience of online shopping, not only discounts, coupons, and special in-store deals become very important, but also salespersons become more highly trained to use behavioral techniques that can increase sales. Although one may believe that salespersons will disappear as brick-and-mortar stores keep closing down, in reality, salespersons will continue to exist and affect business differently. In-store shopping and online shopping are two ways of making purchases that now work in concert. Since customers usually search online before entering the store, the salesperson must be familiar with products available on the store website.

During the two-month pandemic closure of the Neiman Marcus store in Orlando, salespersons continued to sell with company phones, contacting customers, offering deals, showing images of products, and physically ringing up sales with their phones. Clearly, only the most experienced and knowledgeable salespersons did well. Salespersons that couldn't produce sales with their phone were laid off before the store even reopened. Our customers weren't physically shopping in the store, but they were making purchases with the assistance of a store salesperson who knew the merchandise that was available in the store and in the warehouse. These sales were guided sales. Retail employees are essential to the success of a business when they're experienced.

Monetary compensation, even if low, can increase retention. Retail employees know that pay is insufficient in every store and they never assist customers just because of their pay. Hourly wages are low. Commissions are low. Retail jobs have different motivators. Better income can be one of the criteria determining which store to work for. It's quite common for a retail worker to switch to a similar job in another store because the pay is one or two dollars per hour higher or because there is a commission on top of base pay.

Customer service still remains essential, particularly in brick-and-mortar stores. Salespersons aren't alone executing a difficult and exhausting task. Shopping is hard work too. Customers can become irritable or anxious while shopping. In the Dresses department of Lord & Taylor, a customer could try 20 dresses and decide not to buy any of them. Luckily, the store had an excellent alterations department. Small solutions can go a long way. That's when customer service kicks in. The salesperson had to find out what was wrong with the fit of the dresses. Then, with the expertise of a seamstress, she offered solutions. Before I bought my last used car, I didn't like the tinted glass. The salesman told me that he could have the tint removed free of charge. That's when I was ready to buy the car.

In the Swimwear department of Lord & Taylor, some employees complained when customers wanted to try multiple bathing suits. They thought it was an annoying waste of their time. The customer willing to try multiple bathing suits is actually doing a favor to the salesperson. Bathing suits have to solve sensitive problems. The more suits a customer tries, the higher the likelihood of a sale. I used to go to the stockroom to find additional choices and I always ended up with the sale of multiple suits.

Customer service may require working around the rules if it can lead to a sale. For example, in order to close a sale, an employee may place a product on a long-term hold that isn't allowed. Janet, one of my coworkers at Neiman Marcus had a customer who was willing to purchase expensive Jay Strongwater jungle figurines at the lowest possible price. The company had allowed price adjustments of sale items in the past. Since customers were abusing this system, adjusting the price of large amounts of products repeatedly, the company stopped this practice. Discounted products could no longer be discounted. Therefore, since prices dropped three times during sales, waiting for the lowest price was the only option. The risk was losing the product, if it sold out at a higher price. Janet used to hide holds in the stockroom and wait.

"Didn't Mr. Sullivan come in for the tiger?" I would ask her.

"He's coming this weekend. He has been very busy at work, but he's coming in," she would reassure me. A week later, the tiger would still be on hold in the stockroom.

"Did Mr. Sullivan change his mind?" I would ask her.

"No, he's definitely buying it. He just couldn't come last week. He was tied up with work. He'll be here this weekend," Janet would say evasively. As soon as the price dropped, Janet called Mr. Sullivan, who appeared in the store and purchased the tiger at the discounted price he had been waiting for.

At Lord & Taylor, during the holiday season, we had a display of Godiva chocolates. The posted sign indicated that the purchase of a specific box of chocolates entitled the customer to receive an additional free box. One day, a husband and wife approached me. "Is there a limit to the offer? We need to buy numerous gifts," they said. I asked Naomi, an employee in Lingerie.

"I think it's one free box per customer," she replied, but she wasn't really sure. The couple wasn't happy, showing me that the sign didn't specify that the offer was one per customer. The sign clearly stated that the purchase of a specific box of chocolates was matched with a free box of chocolates. Our manager wasn't in the store. After some hesitation, I decided to let them have the offer without limitations. After all, no one had purchased Godiva chocolates for several weeks. Seven different people buying one box or one person buying seven boxes seemed the same to me.

"That's fine," I agreed.

"Now we're in business! You never say no to a customer!" the man told Naomi. She kept quiet and I thought I'd better remember in the future what this man said. The couple purchased numerous boxes of chocolates, looking very satisfied with the free gifts.

"I don't think we're supposed to give away so many free boxes to the same customer," said Naomi after the couple left.

As we were somberly discussing the possible dramatic outcome of this sale, after our manager found out, the couple returned to our department to buy another box of chocolates and get another free box.

"We went over our list of gifts and calculated that we need two more boxes," he said with a smile.

I complied with the customer's request, but aside from being afraid of having broken some arcane rule, I didn't feel that bad. The customers were really happy and the chocolates weren't selling. A week later, our manager gave us instructions.

"Make sure you only give one free box per customer!" she said. Her instructions were one week too late. After the holiday season ended, the price of Godiva chocolates dropped significantly. Employees were buying discounted chocolates with their employee discount on top. I'm still not sure that my sale was wrong. The satisfied customers probably told all their friends what a good store Lord & Taylor was, providing advertisement.

Not all customers come into the store with the intention to buy. Some are just curious. I had a couple of customers who had just arrived in the United States from Italy and were browsing in our Lord & Taylor store. I had a long conversation with them, discovering where they were from, what they were doing in Boca Raton, and how long they were going to stay. I talked to them about our store and went to get a discount coupon for foreigners. At Lord & Taylor, foreigners couldn't open a credit card account and benefit from the initial discount. Therefore, the store provided coupons for foreign tourists. I mentioned that we were going to have a major event three days later and invited them. They left without buying anything, but three days later they appeared in front of my counter. The wife was triumphantly holding the discount coupon in her hand. They were ready to make purchases around the store.

We had food, drinks, and a D.J. to entertain the customers. They loved it. The lady selected multiple items in the Swimwear area. Then, they went to look around the store. They came back holding items from the Men's department. They bought everything from me, absolutely elated about their coupon. No one gives you a discount coupon when you walk into a store or department store in Italy. However, establishing rapport with them is what brought them back to my counter.

It's rewarding to see customers leaving satisfied and returning to the store. A young woman approached me and told me that she had purchased a bathing suit from me at Swim 'n Sport the previous year, before it closed. She was very satisfied with her bathing suit and asked me to assist her with a purchase of sunglasses at Lord & Taylor. I had no recollection of her. Apparently, she was willing to make another purchase in a different store with me. This is probably one of the reasons why one shouldn't work in a competitor's store when one has two jobs.

Although I was building a clientele during the 8-month period in which I worked at Lord & Taylor, I was never able to see the seeds that I planted turn into beautiful blooming flowers. On March 13, 2014, disaster struck. We had a Friends and Family event on that day and sales were going particularly well. While a teenage girl was trying on a few bikinis, her mother asked me for a different size. While I was walking in the direction of the bathing suit rack, I skidded, tried to keep my balance making an awkward movement so that I wouldn't fall, and cracked my left kneecap without even hitting it. This tragic accident catapulted me out of Lord & Taylor into a hospital, and then into a physical rehabilitation center.

The store paid for all my medical expenses, including two surgeries, through workers' compensation. I had no medical insurance and when the ambulance reached the hospital, I was told to go home and come back the next day since it wasn't clear who was going to pay my bills. My apartment was on the second floor and I was still sleeping on an inflatable mattress, on the floor. I didn't get up from my chair in the waiting room. The hospital finally allowed me to check in. My surgery took place two days later, after contact had been made with my workers' compensation adjuster.

Lord & Taylor held my job for one year. I missed my daughter's graduation a few weeks later. After her graduation, she continued to work part-time on campus, until her apartment lease expired. I was in the rehabilitation center for two months. Finally, we moved together into an apartment without stairs, as I was limping and still not climbing stairs easily. My daughter loaded our belongings onto a U-Haul truck and drove both of us to a new apartment complex near Boca Raton. My 21-year-old daughter was truly my hero. Aware of my tragic accident, my ex-husband stopped paying court-ordered alimony. We didn't have enough money to support both of us for a long time. Luckily, my daughter found employment in Orlando. We hired a small local moving company and moved to Orlando.

I still had months of rehabilitation and a second surgery ahead. Eight months later, I had to accept the fact that I financially couldn't go back to my part-time job at Lord & Taylor and that I couldn't handle the physically challenging job at Italio restaurant. When unexpected disaster strikes, low wages and precarious employment no longer suffice. Without alimony, there was no way I could have survived on a part-time job or even two part-time jobs. I applied for a full-time job at Lord & Taylor, but they probably considered me as a liability after my kneecap fracture and didn't allow it. My ex-husband had played his cards well. He wanted me penniless, and in the street, as he had threatened in the past. He had succeeded, but maybe not so fast...

When my workers' compensation ended, I needed to find a job in Orlando quickly. It wasn't easy because I was still a little unstable and afraid of stairs. In fact, I had also subsequently fractured one of my ribs falling off my shower stool. This fracture required a couple of months to heal. I had a job interview in a furniture store interested in hiring me, but I saw a long and steep staircase connecting the two floors of the store which scared me away.

I was hired as a timeshare salesperson by Hilton Grand Vacations. I gained additional sales training. This timeshare sales job was very different from the one I had held at Wyndham Vacation Ownership. The Hilton job was strictly a phone job without resort tours. I was given a list of leads that I was supposed to contact by phone. Most of my phone numbers were bad numbers that couldn't be called. Hilton didn't allow salespersons to close their sales. I had closers who weren't closing any of my sales. In fact, on one occasion, the closer was sitting on a table, throwing paper balls at another employee, while talking with my customer on the phone. He didn't seem very driven to me. Having to rely on a closer was the main reason why I quit this job. The company had hired a group of very capable real estate agents, who were leaving the company one by one. Only one salesperson, hired with my group, was trained and allowed to close his sales because he spoke Spanish. He was assigned Spanish-speaking leads frequently. Right before I left, he told me that he was allowed to close his deals, without having to rely on another person. Therefore, he said he was going to stay longer with the company and see how much money he could make.

In April 2014, Sears hired me as a cashier and fired me during my training period because, as the two firing managers told me, "No one likes you." It was probably good that I lost that job, as the company wasn't functioning well. Its loyalty programs didn't seem to be successful. Customers didn't show an interest in accumulating points redeemable for future purchases. On a Friends and Family shopping day, Sears offered the choice between a 15% discount on the purchase or a high number of points. All customers I assisted at the register picked the immediate discount. Some customers openly voiced their lack of interest in the point system. Sears didn't have enough customer loyalty.

The Sears reward system used to send "surprise points" to its customers through an email. On one occasion a customer with $20 in surprise points, purchased an item that cost $15. As he was about to leave, one of the managers urged him to pick another item with a $5 cost.

"You can have it for free!" she told him and he did.

I heard managers say "You can have it for free!" frequently while I worked at Sears. The prices were already very low and often comparable to those in discount stores. Clearance items, such as jackets, pants, shirts, with a very low price combined with the free point currency system, didn't promote high sales, which is what the store needed.

The use of credit cards allowed customers to accelerate accumulation of points. However, customers didn't seem interested in opening a credit card for this reason. They wanted an immediate discount only. After opening a credit card account, the discount on the first purchase was $15 with the Sears MasterCard and $10 with the basic Sears store card. If the purchase totaled $15, Sears employees used to say: "If you open a Sears credit card account, you can have this item for free." Usually stores offer a percentage discount on the first purchase: the more you spend, the more you save. For Sears it was a free item giveaway. Some cashiers offered to open both Sears cards allowing the customer to receive a $25 discount ($15 for the Sears MasterCard and $10 for the Sears regular card). Customers seemed receptive to this offer. However, $25 is an excessive discount on a purchase below $50.

Through the "Shop Your Way" loyalty program, Sears customers were allowed to process an exchange or return online. After receiving a confirmation email, customers drove to the store and communicated their arrival in the parking lot. Within a few minutes, a Sears associate picked up or exchanged the returned item, while the customer remained inside the vehicle. My orientation trainer highlighted this service as unique because no other store in the United States offered it. In reality, it was a service that kept the customers out of the store, while all stores were and are trying to figure out ways to bring customers into the store and increase sales. A return can be a starting point for a new purchase when a salesperson interacts with the customer inside the store. Sears had low traffic. Discounts and gifts can be good incentives, but if a business is already struggling, they can be harmful.

The store wasn't extremely tidy. I saw roaches walking on the floor, non-functional registers, heavily stained furniture in the office, and lack of garbage bags to line the trash cans at the cash wraps. During the hiring process, they told me that I was randomly chosen to skip the customary drug test, which means that the company was probably trying to save money. During inventory, the skeletal staff was asked to work a crazy schedule. One of the employees, who was a single mother, complained that she had been asked to work from 4 a.m. until lunch time, go home for a couple of hours, and then come back and work until closing. Her elementary school son had to take the bus alone in the morning. She refused to work in the afternoon. Clearly this store didn't use its human resources well and seemed to be scrambling to survive. I wondered many times whether the store had fired me within ten days because it realized that it couldn't afford to pay me. It made no sense to hire me and fire me so quickly during my training period, for no reason. Five years later, the store shut down.

Bloomingdale's offered me a group interview that I didn't pass. The interviewer asked numerous questions trying to identify salespersons who were focusing on customer service. I didn't give the right answers because I didn't verbalize that customer service was my primary focus. I also failed an interview with a bank and with Amscot, a company that provides cash advance services.

Macy's offered me an interview for a furniture sales position. However, my interviewer told me that the company had posted the job incorrectly. The job opening was in the Rug department. I expressed my interest in selling rugs especially after my interviewer said that the store was the largest rug seller in the south. I left the interview feeling certain that I was going to be hired, but no one contacted me. About a week later, I contacted Macy's. I was told that I had to reapply because Macy's had to change the incorrect job posting.

The desperate and continuous search for a suitable job, the dramatic attempt to survive and take care of a family, which in many cases includes little children, the constant changes from one employment to another one due to unexpected circumstances, are all very typical and widespread in retail. I wasn't an extraordinary case. One of my coworkers who had been laid off by Neiman Marcus, hopped from one job to another trying to cover her mortgage and living expenses. She was laid off by Bed Bath &

Beyond when it closed down. She worked two part-time jobs for a while and she currently works in a gift shop. She seems to have settled down in her present job, which satisfies her needs. However, if anything unexpected occurs, she'll be searching for another job again until she can find something suitable. She's persistent and never gives up, like all retail workers who remain on top of the wave. Part-time jobs, multiple jobs, and frequent change of jobs allow these workers to keep paying bills and survive, even if with extreme difficulty. A Walmart employee told me that after finishing his day shift, he worked a night shift in another store. Did he ever sleep? Some employees take naps in the break room. Everyone is constantly looking for money, a stable job, and acceptable living and working conditions.

After being fired by Sears, I was hired to sell a medical alert system by phone, from home. Unexpectedly, before starting my new job, I received a phone call that literally changed my life. Lisa, the manager of Gift Gallery, the home decor department at Neiman Marcus, called me to set up an interview.

"I used to work at Lord & Taylor before it closed down," she told me. I didn't understand what she was saying. Did Lord & Taylor close already? They had just opened the Boca Raton store in 2014.

"I worked for Lord & Taylor years ago, before they closed in Florida," she explained.

She had a good memory of Lord & Taylor and the name of this company on my resume caught her attention. Unlike

San Diego stores that refused to hire the employees laid off by Linens 'n Things, Neiman Marcus in Orlando had been hiring employees laid off by other major companies that had closed down, like Saks and Nordstrom. These employees were usually well-trained, experienced, and used to dealing with high design and difficult customers. For this reason, the store had magnificent employees that contributed significantly to its success. One of its top salespersons had been laid off by Saks. I wasn't a laid off case. I had fractured my kneecap. Lisa understood that I had lost my job outside of my control and also saw in my resume that I was part of the President's Club of Lord & Taylor, which is synonymous with very high sales.

On the day of my interview, I stepped off the escalator on the second floor, but I didn't know where Gift Gallery was. I asked an employee near the escalator if he could direct me. He immediately stopped what he was doing. With extreme politeness, he walked with me to my destination, wishing me good luck on my interview. Later, I would find out that his name was James and that he had been a salesperson in the Men's department of Nordstrom. He had been hired by Neiman Marcus when Nordstrom closed in Orlando. James was now a very good and devoted employee of Neiman Marcus. He was going to become one of my best friends. He was accurate, hard-working, and always ready to do anything that could improve store function. He told me that he was basically the breadwinner of his family. He was very attached to his young nephew.

"He draws very well. When he finishes high school, I'll get a second job if I have to, in order to send him to a design school," James told me about his nephew.

In reality, James wasn't insensitive to design aesthetics either. He used to enter my department with a cart full of boxes and as he opened them to take out the newly arrived products, he expressed his personal admiration.

"Look! This is beautiful!" he used to say, pointing at the details and colors of the vases, platters, statues, figurines he was unwrapping. Then, he placed the products on display tables, paying attention to the lighting.

"That looks so good! You are better than Lukas!" I used to tell him, referring to the store designer who took care of most of the displays in Gift Gallery. James certainly had artistic talent, although he didn't know it. It must have run in his family. James did well. Neiman Marcus always rewarded good, hard-working employees. Eventually, he was promoted within the department in which he worked.

During my job interview, Lisa outlined succinctly how Neiman Marcus conducted its business in a different way from all other stores. If retail requires passion for customer service, this axiom is what defined the identity of Neiman Marcus, due to the way its business was structured. Lisa told me what to expect in general terms. I was going to figure out on my own how to work in a store that did a large amount of its business building loyal customers with a company phone.

Lisa hired me as a full-time employee with a pay of $10/hour, which would have been enough for me to accept, plus a commission of 2% on sales. A few years later, my hourly base pay was raised to $12/hour, as Neiman Marcus was competing with other major retailers hiring employees at that rate. I had a very generous packet of benefits, which included a magnificent health insurance. Every year, the company paid for a full health screening. Smoke-free employees like me received a significant discount on their health insurance. This means that the portion deducted from our paycheck was much lower. Lisa indicated that I had to open a minimum of two credit card accounts a month. The company paid $10 for each new credit card. It was and will remain the highest pay I ever received in a retail store.

Neiman Marcus paid its salespersons very well because they developed a very loyal clientele and brought in the sales. Lisa added that I was going to receive an iPhone to conduct business and develop clients. The minimum sales amount I had to generate during my first year was $100,000. Lisa walked me through the department and showed me the stockroom which was on two floors. I looked at the stockroom stairs with horror, tightly holding the handrail as we climbed up and came back down. It was my chance to overcome my fears and start using stairs on a regular basis. A few months later, I was going up and down those stairs holding crystals, heavy books, tabletop items, etc.

The following hiring steps were to take the drug test and then meet with the human resources representative, who was going to give me the phone and more information. I left the interview feeling very happy. The pay was amazing, the job was excellent, the store looked spectacular, and my manager seemed very nice and knowledgeable. She turned out to be phenomenal.

Strangely, I continued to miss Lord & Taylor as time passed. During the seven years spent at Neiman Marcus, every day I brought to work a large canvas bag showcasing the Lord & Taylor logo, which the company had given to all employees to carry necessities. It was a way to keep me emotionally tied to the company where I had planned to become a manager. The Neiman Marcus general manager noticed my Lord & Taylor bag one day.

"We'll have to distribute some Neiman Marcus bags to all employees," she said, jokingly.

The store ended up giving us a large pouch with the Neiman Marcus logo. I used that pouch to keep my business cards, pens, orders information, receipts to follow shipments, and other items. However, I placed my pouch inside the Lord & Taylor bag, which I still have in my possession. It took me a long time to truly open up to Neiman Marcus, a company that had offered me more than a lifeline. I don't know why I could never completely break my bond with Lord & Taylor, a company that had refused to give me a full-time job from the day of hiring and had assigned to my department a manager who didn't seem supportive. I did embrace the Neiman Marcus culture and business completely from a rational and practical standpoint. I truly devoted all my time and skills to this company. It paid off.

6

Portrait of a Store

While my attachment to Lord & Taylor deeply filled my heart with conflicting emotions, every day I couldn't help but notice the artistic nature of the new company that had opened its doors to me. Art has always been an important presence in my family's life. My parents were art collectors. My mother was a successful painter and ceramist. Since childhood, I was taught to respect and appreciate the beauty of all art forms. I was now working for a very artistic store, in which design and aesthetics ruled majestically.

All the paintings decorating the walls of the store had been made by famous local artists. Some of the tables used to display merchandise were artworks. In Gift Gallery, we had a large wooden table with interesting inlays. Many customers asked to purchase that table over the years, but it was a store fixture. Some of the chandeliers were also unusual. Above the escalator connecting the two floors, hundreds of paper butterflies were hung from the ceiling with invisible threads. The butterflies sparkled slightly as they moved. All customers used to ride the escalator with their head pointed upwards, looking at the butterflies. Everyone felt the magic that this store was exuding from every corner. Lukas, the store designer, contributed to the beauty of each department with his stunning floral compositions. I was immersed in a spectacular setting, created by the artistic interaction of lights, shapes, and colors.

Customers frequently professed their love for Neiman Marcus. When the company filed for Chapter 11 bankruptcy in 2020, they texted me frequently asking about the status of their favorite store.

"I wouldn't want to see this store close. I love Neiman Marcus!" they used to tell me as they placed one order after another through the phone. In 20 years of retail, I have never seen such powerful customer loyalty and passion for a store.

Neiman Marcus had a personal character that made it unique. It sold unusual products, sometimes handmade and hand-painted in other countries. One year, we had a trunk show of African art. It included large ceramic sculptures and textiles, such as table runners, table cloths, and cushions. I advertised the upcoming trunk show multiple times, starting one month prior to its arrival in the store. Finally, our department was filled with beautiful handmade Ardmore ceramic sculptures: elephants, crocodiles, giraffes, frogs, leopards, zebras, hippos, and monkeys. There were also vases, teapots, platters and other objects decorated with 3D animal and human figurines. We had an amazing turnout of customers. Some of them had been to Africa and were familiar with Ardmore ceramics. Since each piece was a unique work of art, they made many purchases.

Neiman Marcus is the most international store I ever worked for. The break room looked like a gathering place for United Nations representatives. A group of Russian speaking employees spoke Russian at one table; a group of French employees spoke French at another table; a group of Spanish speaking employees occupied another corner. If a group spoke English, most salespersons had a very strong foreign accent. Elena, one of the salespersons in the Beauty department, told us a funny episode about her accent. When she was hired years earlier, her English was difficult to comprehend. One of the customers asked Elena's manager if she could have a different salesperson. The manager refused to change the salesperson and asked Elena to continue communicating, regardless of her strong accent. Neiman Marcus was notorious for its different accents. A manager told me that these accents weren't accidental. The fact that employees were from all over the world wasn't unintentional. I loved the multi-ethnic atmosphere of Neiman Marcus. Customers were charmed and intrigued by the exotic atmosphere created by its employees.

Internationalism promoted sales and cooperation. We worked well together, accepting our differences. I started interacting with a Japanese salesperson because I frequently needed help in her Beauty area. We became friends. Eventually, I informed her when we had a sale of imported Japanese foods in my department. She was thrilled with the sale and bought many products. Then, she showed up with other Asian salespersons who were interested in Japanese foods. Soon, I had a group of customers within the store, who wanted to be alerted when new Asian foods arrived or went on sale. They always helped me when I went to their Beauty sections, looking for products or samples for my customers, which increased their brand sales. I also asked them to ring me up when I made a purchase. It was a good mutual business relationship.

I always thought that I was privileged to work in Gift Gallery because of the ever-changing variety of its interesting products. Fine apparel surely had beautiful clothes of luxury designer brands from overseas. The Handbags, Shoes, and Jewelry departments also had products made by amazing American and foreign designers. However, Gift Gallery was truly unique. We had products made by permanent designers and also arrivals of special artworks.

When James showed up with his cart full of boxes, he often found me texting in an empty department.

"Did you also bring some customers in that cart?" I used to ask him.

"No, but look how beautiful!" he quickly reverted my attention to the amazing products he started unwrapping. We always ended up commenting together, "Wow!" "This is gorgeous!" "The colors are incredible!" "Fantastic design!" James and I shared an appreciation for art. There were times when I was busy communicating with a customer by phone and I couldn't witness the unwrapping of new products. However, James used to come back later and show me everything he had brought and where he had placed the products in the stockroom.

Neiman Marcus had the most liberal dress code I encountered in all my years in retail. Each department had slightly different rules, but generally women wore dresses or skirts with jackets or cardigans. Rarely, some women wore dressy slacks. Men had to wear jackets, but they could skip their tie. Women were allowed to wear any color, and they didn't have to cover their shoulders as Macy's required. I loved being able to choose the colors of my dresses, skirts, and tops. I often thought I was lucky I hadn't been hired by Bloomingdale's, which required an entirely black dress code. Long dresses weren't allowed because the store didn't want salespersons to trip when going up or down the escalator. However, we had the freedom to personalize our outfits. Most salespersons told me that they purchased their designer dresses in discount stores. I did the same and also purchased them online. We all looked fabulous on a budget.

Women wore all types of shoes, including flat sandals, strappy sandals, thong sandals, gladiator sandals, wedge sandals, open shoes, closed shoes, open-toe, strapped or unstrapped shoes. The store didn't care. The only requirement was refined presence. Every component of the outfit had to be elegant and preferably trendy. Comfort ruled because salespersons were in the store to make money and not just look like pretty models. Newly hired women had a tendency to wear high heels. As time went on, they started wearing more comfortable shoes. I had to go up and down the stairs of the stockroom all day, cross the store frequently, go to the Shipping department and back to my area, and carry heavy boxes. Therefore, I opted for dressy flat sandals in the summer and stylish boots with a low heel in the winter. If we had a corporate visit coming up in the store, our manager would remind us to dress particularly well for the occasion. We used to arrive at the store wearing high heels, but as soon as the visitor left, we switched to more comfortable shoes.

When I first started working at Neiman Marcus, salespersons assisted customers in their own areas. If a customer asked for assistance in a different department, they could do so. If they weren't knowledgeable in the other department, they could get help from the salesperson in that area and then split the sale. However, split sales weren't as common as one would think because salespersons generally don't like splitting sales. Therefore, they helped employees from other areas without taking half of the sale. I did the same thing. When salespersons from other areas came to Gift Gallery, I helped them find products and shared information, but I never split the sale. I wanted my sales to be entirely mine.

My first coworker in Gift Gallery was Tanya, who was known for taking other people's sales. I had been hired to replace Robin, who had asked to be transferred out of Gift Gallery because, as she explained to me, she was tired of Tanya interrupting her sales and taking over her customers. If a salesperson from another department came to our area to place a sale and asked for help, Tanya always split the sale, which was legitimate, but not conducive to good friendships in the store. If Tanya wasn't busy, she always started talking to my customers to take over my sale. I complained to Lisa, but she didn't take action. Neiman Marcus managers generally didn't intervene in sales disputes. Split sales or switched sales occurred only when both salespersons turned in a signed request.

"It's a grey area," my manager's manager David said about sales disputes.

Eventually, a few years later, Tanya started taking the customers of a third coworker named Shelley. Jennifer, my second manager, had hired Shelley and wasn't happy about her complaints. No manager took action. Finally, Tanya moved out of state for personal reasons. Jennifer clearly indicated that she would never allow Tanya to come back to our department in the future. We were all happy to be rid of her.

Usually, I managed to get sales only when Tanya was busy. She had the habit of chatting with her customers for a long time. This allowed me to assist multiple walk-in customers. In my first year, I had a lucky sale during Tanya's lunch break. A South American woman walked into our department and purchased about $30,000 of merchandise to decorate her new home in Orlando. This woman never became a loyal customer of mine. She shopped infrequently, she never announced her intention to come to the store, and she never interacted with me properly. I was lucky to catch her a couple of times when she made even larger purchases than the first time. During her second visit to my department, she spent about $70,000.

On one occasion, she purchased a very expensive Jay Strongwater crystal-decorated floral table for her porch. This table was delivered with a cracked glass top, but we found out about the damage many months later. The woman who had been hired to take care of her Orlando house while she was in her home country, turned out to be careless. She organized lavish personal parties in this house and didn't check deliveries. If she made a purchase for her boss during a store gift card event, she kept the gift card for herself. My communication with the South American customer was difficult and fragmented. As she returned from one of her trips abroad, the Strongwater table was finally unwrapped and found to be damaged. Getting the glass piece replaced wasn't easy, due to the delay in discovering the damage. My managers allowed the replacement only because the customer spent thousands of dollars each time she showed up in our store. However, she came to our store less and less often. After the Covid outbreak started, I heard from her maintenance woman, who also shopped in our store, that the house caretaker had been fired. I never saw the South American customer again.

Foreign tourists usually paid with prepaid cards or personal cards, whereas regular customers preferred the Neiman Marcus store card to take advantage of the card benefits. American Express had some very loyal cardholders, who preferred to use their own card, disregarding the benefits of the Neiman Marcus store card, even if they were repetitive customers. Mrs. Lansing, in particular, consistently refused to apply for a Neiman Marcus credit card. She bought very expensive products, which would have allowed her to receive many points to be redeemed for gift cards. As I kept insisting that she should have applied for the store card, she finally decided to come to our store to shop and open an account. Some of her family members drove with her from Daytona Beach to our Orlando store. Mrs. Lansing picked her products and when she was ready to pay and open her credit card account, the store credit card system stopped working. It was a terribly embarrassing situation because this customer had come to our store specifically to apply for the store card and pay with it. She continued to shop with her American Express for years and I resigned myself to the impossibility of getting her a store card. She could have applied for the Neiman Marcus credit card online, but she wasn't comfortable inputting her personal information online. She trusted me enough to give me her American Express card number by telephone, each time she made a purchase. She never allowed me to save her card number.

The Children's department was adjacent to Gift Gallery. The two areas were managed by the same manager. When I started working at Neiman Marcus, Julie and Sara were the two salespersons in the Children's area. They had been working together for over ten years. In order to prevent competition, they split all their sales when they both worked in the store. If one of them was off, the other salesperson took the sales of that day, with some exceptions. Regular customers in the Children's department dealt with both of them interchangeably. A few customers were particularly loyal to Julie and requested to shop with her only. When they had no customers to assist, Julie and Sara spent a long time deciding which sales belonged to whom, with receipts in hand. They had to fill out and sign forms requesting the split payment. After Sara retired, Julie realized how much more money she was making alone, even though the store had hired a new salesperson.

"I'll never split my sales again," she used to say, but she did miss Sara after working with her for so many years.

All employees walked around the store holding their phone and texting customers. Initially, the phone caused me some anxiety because I really didn't know what to do with it. In the break room, I asked some employees about their phone use.

"I use the phone to send pictures of products and get orders. That's how I make my money. I have over 600 customers to text," replied one salesperson.

"How do you text so many people?" I asked.

"I know my main ones. Depending on the products and the events, I choose which customers to text," she explained, holding the phone tightly in her hands.

I didn't have hundreds of customers and it didn't take me very long to realize that the store had very little foot traffic in my area. What I didn't know yet was that the store had very intense traffic through the phone. Customers placed hundreds of orders through the phone, without coming to the store very often.

We were encouraged by the managers to use the phone to advertise store products on social media, after taking a brief course. The instructor taught us what we weren't allowed to do while posting pictures. I chose to advertise on Instagram, which to my surprise gave me a huge number of followers from the very beginning. However, Instagram didn't bring in sales. No one ever contacted me to ask to purchase a product I featured on Instagram. Other employees in other departments confirmed that Instagram never generated sales for them either. It only seemed to give visibility to the company. What gave us sales was really texting customers directly.

Initially, since I had few customers and abundant downtime, I often took pictures and prepared Instagram postings. Gradually, as the number of my customers increased, my Instagram postings decreased and stopped almost completely. Six years later, I was assisting customers in the store, simultaneously working on a couple of sales on the phone. How did this crazy multi-tasking activity take place? I used to take requests and pull products while the in-store shoppers were browsing. I communicated with customers on the phone while I was getting products in the stockroom. If I was really busy with an in-store customer, I sent my typical text message: "I'll be back ASAP." My customers knew what it meant and they patiently waited for me to resume texting. If I received a phone order for an item that was the last one available in the warehouse, I would quickly rush to place the order on the register while the in-store customer was busy.

Men browsers required closer attention than women because they were very targeted shoppers, who entered the store to purchase a specific item and then walked out. Generally, they didn't seem interested in acquiring products that weren't of immediate need. Instead, women were usually ready to explore unplanned solutions for their home decor. When a couple shopped together, if the woman's attention was drawn to a particular object, invariably the man asked her: "Do you really need that?" Most men bought mainly what they believed they needed. Women had a very wide shopping scope. Women shopping with a spouse were somewhat limited as compared to women shopping alone. Although the nesting instinct is attributed solely to expectant mothers, I believe that women have a nesting instinct throughout their entire life. It may become more pronounced during pregnancy. Wise men are agreeable when their women shop because inhibiting their desire to stock their homes goes against their nature.

On my first day of work, Lisa took me on a tour of the entire department, giving me relevant information about each designer we carried. She expected me to know this basic information in order to be able to assist the customers. Macy's West is the only other store in which the manager took me on a department tour, showing and describing to me the features of the displayed products. The next day, Lisa took me on a second tour of the department. This time, she asked me to repeat everything that I remembered about each designer. Although I missed a few details that she quickly filled in, she seemed satisfied. Then, she gave me a binder that she had put together with printed information about most designers in the store, including minor ones she had not talked about. She urged me to study during my downtime. Finally, she also encouraged me to go online and research any designer information not featured in the binder or not discussed during our department tour.

I followed Lisa's instructions during all the years I worked for Neiman Marcus. If I saw a name engraved on a Baccarat platter, I searched online whose name it was. If I encountered an art form that I was unfamiliar with, such as John Derian's decoupage, I made sure I studied online what it involved. Lisa also kept designers' catalogs going back many years in time. If a customer asked for a specific Jay Strongwater figurine or a plate from an old Juliska collection, I could look them up and search if they were still available in another store. Sometimes, I could ask Lisa to request products from the vendor. Unfortunately, after Lisa left, her binder with designer information and most designer pamphlets were thrown away.

My first year at Neiman Marcus required a tremendous amount of knowledge acquisition, but I had an exceptional manager who trained all employees in a superb manner and skillfully controlled every aspect of her "complex area," as she used to define it. Gift Gallery was a very difficult area that required experience, a very proactive attitude, and a manager present most of the time. After working in Gift Gallery for several years, I had the advantage of having handled products that we no longer carried in the store, but that were still available to order. A salesperson waiting for a walk-in customer, without researching products nor establishing strong bonds with buyers, realistically didn't sell. As a bonus, Lisa also gave me the names and phone numbers of some customers who had lost their salespersons.

Lisa never spoke unnecessarily. She was always busy at her desk, which was in the stockroom. As all starting employees, I made foolish errors. Each time I made a mistake, I thought I was going to get fired. Instead, Lisa taught me how to fix the problem, never losing her composure or making judgmental comments. Each time I made a mistake, I learned never to repeat it again.

We started receiving Christmas ornaments, collectibles, and decorations at the end of August and Lisa displayed the merchandise because it started selling immediately. Labor Day attracted many customers. The Gift Gallery managers that later replaced Lisa, used to hold Christmas products in the stockroom until the end of October, which was a mistake in my opinion. Not only we had local residents ready to purchase early in the season or looking for collectibles before they sold out, but we also had tourists from other countries who came to our store in the summer and purchased ornaments, nutcrackers and more. I bubble-wrapped them and the customers brought them back to their countries in their suitcases. A Scottish customer bought a humorous and very large Mackenzie Childs deer head to hang in her kitchen. The following year, she came back to our department in the summer and bought an even larger moose head. Although I bubble-wrapped it well, I questioned whether she could take it overseas.

"Are you going to be able to take it with you? Would you like me to ship it to you?"

"If she could take the deer head last year, she'll manage to take the moose!" said her confident husband. And indeed, they succeeded in taking all their purchases to Scotland with their suitcase. Every year, they came back during the summer, but when our manager changed, we no longer had any Christmas products on display.

During my first Christmas season, I made my first horrible mistake. A local customer purchased a large amount of Jay Strongwater ornaments, as well as other decorative items. The Strongwater ornaments we had in the store were displayed on a Strongwater metal tree, which was also for sale. I took products from the stockroom and I also opened one of the drawers where I saw Strongwater ornament boxes, taking one of the boxes from there. The customer paid and left in the most positive mood. The following day, I saw Tanya take a box out of the drawer to fill it with the last ornament of its kind displayed on the tree. I discovered that the boxes in the drawer were all empty. My heart sank. I walked into the stockroom and without holding back my anxiety, I went straight to Lisa.

"Oh my God! I did something terrible! I made a horrible mistake!" She looked at me very attentively, without flinching. "Yesterday I sold an empty box that was in the drawer. I thought the boxes of Strongwater ornaments were full." Lisa didn't reproach me, but gave me clear instructions.

"Count how many ornaments of the same type are on the tree and how many empty boxes are in the drawer." I obediently proceeded to count.

"We have an extra ornament with no box," I reported somberly. I didn't get fired. She never lost her temper. She just told me what to do. I called Mrs. Madison and asked her to check if the box I gave her was empty. She didn't know if she was missing an ornament because she wasn't planning to open the boxes for 2-3 months. She checked and the box was empty.

"I will overnight the ornament to you now" I told her, apologizing for my mistake. The problem was solved, but I learned never to sell or ship any box without opening it and checking its contents.

If I ever become a manager, I'd like to be like Lisa, I frequently thought. I never intended to become a Neiman Marcus manager, but I always thought that she was the ideal manager. She was prompt, precise, organized, and in control. She never lost her temper and always gave excellent direction. If a salesperson didn't reach her goal, she let that employee go according to store procedures. Emotions didn't get in the way. Lisa gave me all the tools I needed to succeed. She solved mistakes and took care of business. The sale numbers ruled. We had sales goals and she was there to help us reach them.

While the store kept me extremely busy on the clock and off the clock, I never spent too much time worrying about my first $100,000 goal. I truly didn't believe it was attainable and I completely disregarded it, focusing instead on learning, taking photos, texting events, posting on Instagram, contacting customers, placing sales, and monitoring shipments. I was certain that the following year I would have had to look for a new job. After all the tough times I had gone through in the past, I never really worried and accepted my fate. I enjoyed my ride and hoped for the best. Years later, $100,000 would turn out to be a very low amount that Neiman Marcus expected from me. Each year, I exceeded my goal and the company gave me an even higher goal. As I voiced my concern for a very high goal, David, my manager's manager, used to say:

"You set that goal for yourself!" He meant that since I exceeded my goal, the following year I ended up with a higher number than the one the company would have given me.

During my first year, I casually developed a method to secure customers and reach my goal. Each time a person walked into the store and placed an order that required a shipment, I used a contact system that established a secure link with that customer. Most orders required a shipment because I placed many orders from the warehouse and because many out of state customers couldn't take the merchandise with them even if it was present in the store. With my phone, I thanked the customers for their orders and sent the tracking number and delivery date (although the customers were going to receive them directly from the system). I tracked all my shipments daily and contacted the customers to communicate any change of delivery date. I contacted the customers to communicate when the package had been delivered. I asked the customers to inspect the product to check if it had arrived in good condition. Finally, I asked how it matched and looked in their house. Most of my texts required a reply. Therefore, I was starting a two-way communication with the customers. If the customers had purchased multiple items and had multiple shipments, since the products often arrived from different locations, my texts would multiply. I had to text tracking numbers and delivery dates for various products. Very few salespersons went out of their way to text so many times for each shipment. They just assumed that the customers were going to receive the tracking numbers and could follow their shipments on their own.

The customers loved my follow-ups. They felt that I was truly assisting them step by step. If I communicated the delivery of a package and the package wasn't found, the customer asked for my help. I immediately took action to locate where and when the package had been left, according to store procedures. If a package arrived damaged or was lost, I immediately started working on its replacement. Each shipment allowed me to establish a bond with my customers. They knew that with me they could count on superb care and follow-up. They didn't need to track their packages because I did it for them. They didn't need to check if the delivery of a package had changed because I would notify them promptly. They checked outside their door as soon as I told them that their package had been delivered. They didn't need to worry if something went wrong because I promptly took action to replace the merchandise. Customers gradually became dependent on me because they knew that each time they made a purchase from me, they received thorough assistance. Therefore, they continued to place their orders with me.

Shipments turned out to be an excellent way to establish a tight bond after an order. Customers kept my number in their phone and quickly discovered that they could contact me at any time with any question. This was a huge accomplishment considering that many of my customers didn't live in Orlando. Some were from out of state. They just happen to have walked into our store to make a purchase. Afterwards, they continued to receive my texts or started soliciting my texts. They asked for product information or placed another order through the phone. Some customers were so satisfied with the Orlando service that they contacted me for purchases rather than going to the Neiman Marcus store in or near their town. They chose not to place an order with a salesperson they didn't know, who may not have communicated as thoroughly as I did. I constantly shipped products out of state or out of town. I had a few customers from Tampa who drove to our Orlando store because, as they explained, they didn't like the customer service they received in their store.

One of my early customers was from Maine. She had a mother who lived in Florida and came to visit her during the holiday season. The first time I met her in our store, she bought a wreath for her mother and many other items for herself, among which was a set of Baccarat glasses. This set of glasses, as I noticed, didn't have the Baccarat name laser-etched on the base. Since I was new, I hardly thought anything of it and didn't mention it. The wreath eventually was replaced with a larger wreath, which required phone communication and texting. A year later, the customer opened her box of Baccarat glasses. She was upset when she noticed that the Baccarat name wasn't etched on the base. Clearly, she hadn't checked the product within the time limit allowed for exchanges. The glasses were authentic, but the customer wanted all her glasses to have that particular Baccarat marking. I was able to exchange the set of glasses with my manager's authorization and I truly gained a loyal customer who knew I wasn't just trying to get the sale, but also wanted her to be satisfied. Afterwards, if I texted this customer, she paid attention and made purchases promptly.

"I'll take it," "Yes," Send me one!" were typical replies to my texts, if the customers didn't need additional information.

We worked around the clock.

"I place orders all the time, after I leave the store. Sometimes, even at 11 p.m.," Jeffrey told me. He was one of the top salespersons.

I took my phone everywhere. While grocery shopping on my day off, the phone used to ring or receive a text message with an order. I stopped my grocery cart, answered questions, checked if and where a requested product was available, and called the online store to place the order immediately. After the Covid outbreak started, we had the ability to ring up customers with our phone, without contacting the online store. Each store received credit for the sales placed by its salespersons that way. The more time I invested into my work, the more money I made. I used my days off to research products, prepare text messages to send to hundreds of customers, and check shipments.

We truly had all types of customers. They weren't all very wealthy. Some customers shopped in our store for products that they couldn't find anywhere else, such as Mackenzie Childs products. The Mackenzie Childs crowd, which was more like a group of serious cult followers, came from all over the world. American customers, European customers, South American customers, Eastern European customers, and Middle Eastern customers systematically came to our store to buy Mackenzie Childs products, which were shipped in containers to their countries or were lavishly bubble-wrapped by me to be taken inside their suitcases.

Local customers came into the store to buy Mackenzie Childs because products with the courtly check pattern aren't identical. Customers were very picky about colors, finishes, and prints. I had British customers who sent me email messages with a list of products to be placed on hold, shortly before their arrival in Orlando. Harrods in London sold Mackenzie Childs, but at a much higher price. We had one small retailer in Orlando competing with us. This store sold basic Mackenzie Childs products and often had discounts. Eventually it went out of business, and we became the uncontested sellers of Mackenzie Childs. Although one could still purchase a tea kettle or a few other products at a local kitchen store, no one had as wide a selection as we did.

During my first year, Lisa organized a Mackenzie Childs event in our department. Rebecca Proctor, the head designer of the company came to our store with a large trunk show. The success of this event was remarkable. All salespersons throughout the store invited their customers. An enormous crowd showed up. I still didn't have many customers at that time. However, during the event, I captured some walk-ins who became permanent customers of mine.

Our clientele included celebrities, such as lawyers who had worked on high-profile cases, actors, and professional athletes. When a famous person entered our store, our general manager used to email the entire facility, reminding us to treat these guests like regular customers, without staring at them and without taking their picture.

The Children's department attracted customers looking for children's designer clothes. Over the years, more and more famous brands were added. We sold Versace, Dolce & Gabbana, Givenchy, Burberry, UGG, Off-White, Geox, Balenciaga, just to name a few. Occasionally, a group of four or five men, all wearing the same large gold chains and gold grillz came to shop for children's designer clothes. Some salespersons suggested that they were rappers or maybe wealthy gang members. No one could verify their identity because they never shared their personal information.

Many men spent lavishly in the Children's department paying with cash. They didn't allow us to add them into the computer system. If they were forced to surrender their name and address for a shipment, they gave us somebody else's name and address. Sometimes, they called a friend or relative to get an exact shipment address, which was supposed to be their address. Some of them contacted the mother of the children to show the merchandise using their phones, getting opinions on colors and styles. They displayed genuine happiness for the arrival of a newborn or for an upcoming birthday party, but social status remained their primary concern while making their purchases. They carried tall stacks of dollar bills, held together with rubber bands. They used to throw these packs of money into the Neiman Marcus shopping bags, after making their purchases. One day, Julie was worried that the money was visible.

"Put these clothes on top!" she told the shopper, hiding the money under his purchases.

"Yes, much better! You don't want it to look conspicuous," I added as I was standing behind the counter. He laughed, surprised at our customer care, although I'm sure he would have been able to defend himself if anyone tried to burglarize him. He probably didn't even care much about those stacks of money, which may have been the tip of his iceberg.

On another occasion, a salesperson told us about a customer asking for help to find his money.

"I can't find my shopping bag! I have $20,000 in it!" he said.

The employee looked everywhere until she finally found the bag on the floor, near a register. The customer was very grateful because he needed the money to continue shopping. He offered a high monetary compensation to her, which she couldn't take, according to company rules. We all laughed when she told us this story and fantasized about telling the customer that the bag hadn't been found in order to split the money inside. It was a very funny joke. We were all extremely honest and used to dealing with very sensitive information on a daily basis. No one would have ever taken that stack of dollar bills.

The Children's department was always a place where the unexpected happened. One day, a couple of women were arguing about the price of the baby clothing they were buying. They started insulting each other and throwing hangers at each other. Finally, one of them left and the other one continued to shop. David came out of his office to inquire about the argument. He had been alerted by the Loss Prevention employees, who constantly monitored the entire store. Whenever there was an argument or a confrontation, everyone kept a distance because it was a potentially dangerous situation.

We had very honest customers, but also thieves. Our company didn't allow security tags on the merchandise. Therefore, theft was constant.

"There are empty hangers and missing Versace clothes on the rack! The clothes were there this morning!" or "There is a pile of empty hangers abandoned behind that table!" were cries of horror after a theft.

Loss Prevention caught most of them, but not all of them. Once, while standing in Gift Gallery, I saw a little child in the Children's department putting merchandise inside a shopping bag, while his mother pretended to be browsing. I immediately approached them and asked if they wanted to pay for the items in the bag. The mother took the items out of the bag and yelled at her child, who stared at her with a blank expression on his face. Cases of mothers who used their children to steal weren't uncommon.

On another occasion, a woman with a couple of relatives browsed in the Children's department and picked up a designer top. She said she wanted to look around the store and pay elsewhere, which was a red flag. I was also going to lose my commission on the item, if it was going to be rung up in another department without my number. I followed the woman with my eyes as she walked out of the Children's department and, at the same time, I called Rick, the Loss Prevention manager who started following her with his camera. Going down the escalator, the woman opened one of her shopping bags and put the top inside. I called Loss Prevention again.

"I caught her on camera," said Rick. At the end of my shift, I walked towards the Loss Prevention area because our lockers were there and our bags had to be checked before we left the store. I passed the relatives of the thief sitting outside Loss Prevention, waiting. The husband recognized me.

"How long will it take? When is my wife coming out?" he asked me. "I can pay for the top!" he said.

It was too late. The man hadn't grasped the gravity of the situation. He thought that the Loss Prevention manager was just having a talk with his wife. A policeman was already with her. She was going to come out of the Loss Prevention office, handcuffed and escorted by the police. She was going to spend the night in jail. It was ridiculous how these people ruined their life for a children's designer top that they could actually afford to buy!

"That was a good call," said Rick after the ordeal was over. He was happy when he apprehended a thief. I couldn't believe I actually helped him catch a thief! Rick was a tall and athletic young man. Every once in a while, we saw him running across the store towards the entrance to the mall, chasing someone. It was like watching an action movie! On the Loss Prevention counter, he posted pictures of thieves that hadn't been arrested. He expected us to recognize them if they came back to the store. It reminded me of the pictures we kept under the register at Linens 'n Things. I never saw any of these people or if I saw them, I probably didn't recognize them.

After working for a couple of years with Lisa, who managed Gift Gallery in the most efficient manner, we were casually informed that she had been promoted to the Jewelry manager position. We had a new manager coming from the Shoes department. It was a shock for my coworkers, who had worked with Lisa for many years. I was used to losing my hiring manager and accepted the change without fuss. I was lucky to have been able to keep Lisa for almost two years. This managerial replacement marked the beginning of a series of changes that was going to modify Gift Gallery entirely.

7

Did You Say Something?

Communication is truly at the basis of any successful business. Salespersons listen to customers expressing their needs, desires, and complaints. Customers listen to salespersons' suggestions. Managers listen to employees asking for a change when something isn't working well. Employees listen to managers for guidance. Employees listen to other employees learning ways to improve their performance. Everyone listens and communicates. Lack of communication and disregard for a problem create resentment, annoyance, and exasperation. Leaving problems unsolved can hurt a business. An unhappy customer stops shopping. An unhappy employee stops listening to his leaders and possibly resigns. Everyone loses, especially the company.

Yet, within a scenario of failed communication, salespersons tend to be very resilient. They're stubborn go-getters. They work around the rules and get their sales any way they can. If a problem can't be solved due to their manager's lack of intervention or to their coworkers' lack of team play, they won't try to change the system. They don't have time to waste. They often adapt to a problematic situation because ultimately, customers are their only priority. However, problems remain unsolved.

Good communication creates a pleasant work environment in which everyone supports each other with some give and take. It's never a perfect system. David was right when he used to say that a sales dispute is "a grey area." Trying to make things right isn't always simple and that's why managers usually didn't try to resolve a sales dispute. If the two salespersons couldn't work things out on their own, the disagreement remained unsettled. Some salespersons moved to a different department for this reason. Other ones accepted a system that was far from faultless.

After Jennifer replaced Lisa in Gift Gallery, several problems occurred due to lack of proper communication. Jennifer was a good manager with a unique and creative personality, who controlled our department as efficiently as possible. Unlike Lisa, she was very outspoken and managed with a down-to-earth approach. On my first day of work with her, I found her sitting on the sales floor, embracing a tall Waterford crystal vase with her left arm and holding the phone with her right hand.

"I haven't measured it, but I would say that this sucker is at least 12 inches tall," she told the customer.

I was taken aback not just because she didn't give the precise height of the vase to the customer, but because she called it "sucker." Soon, I learned that many other products she referred to were "suckers." She really cared for the products and never meant to be disrespectful towards any of them, but she treated them very informally.

Jennifer had a loud laughter that filled our department. She walked in and out of the stockroom taking charge in the most unceremonious way. Although initially she didn't know much about the brands and products sold in Gift Gallery, she learned fast. She was an experienced manager who did all she could to grow the business in the new area assigned to her. Most of all, she communicated with Lisa, accepting her suggestions and help, when needed.

Jennifer introduced new ideas while managing. For children's shoes, she adopted the same stocking procedures used in the adult Shoe department. She also reorganized the drawers under the display shelves where many shoes were stocked.

She was extremely efficient. This became apparent during our annual inventory, for which she started preparing early. She cleverly utilized what I used to call the "corner of death." There was a recessed area between the Children's department and Gift Gallery, which was consistently bypassed by the browsers. Each store has a characteristic flow of customers walking in the same direction. This flow can be partially controlled by the placement of products throughout a department, but it's also determined by the layout of the floor. Our customers had a tendency to follow the same browsing route, usually skipping the alcove between the two departments. For a while, we had books displayed in this recessed area. Customers loved to spend time quietly leafing through the pages. However, the books didn't attract enough customer attention. Jennifer decided to replace the books with other products. I told her that customers would miss these products.

"That's the corner of death! Anything that you put there doesn't sell!"

Jennifer decided to turn the alcove into a Children's department destination, specifically the Newborn section. If anyone asked where newborn clothes and products were, we would immediately point to the alcove, where products started selling very well. Now the "corner of death" was a place of busy traffic. The drawback was that Gift Gallery had lost some display space. As the company had decided to invest in the Children's department, which was a growing business area, more and more children's brands and products started entering the store. Gradually, Gift Gallery was going to be significantly reduced in size.

Jennifer had a display method that proved to be quite effective, especially during the holiday sales.

"We place popular items in the front and less popular items in the back," she explained. Therefore, Jay Strongwater remained in the best visual position. Customers walking in front of our department couldn't miss the unmistakable sparkle of Strongwater objects covered with crystals. Customers entering the second floor and walking in the direction of the escalator or elevator to go to the first floor, passed the Strongwater shelves and generally stopped to browse. Customers who had never seen Strongwater products were enchanted by their crystal sparkle and made unplanned purchases. I still remember a young man who walked in front of the Strongwater vitrine and was drawn by the sparkle of its products. He asked me about these products, which he wasn't familiar with, and purchased a figurine for his old aunt. As he explained, it was going to be a very special gift because his aunt had raised him when he was a child.

Mackenzie Childs products were moved to a different area of the front. Michael Aram products were in a front room, which used to be the Mackenzie Childs room, extending from the front to the back of the department, although the Children's department was starting to erode this area. Frames that weren't Strongwater frames were grouped together in the back. Frames were also a customer destination. Food was a big seller. Many people liked to browse and find unusual food products. Food products were now located on shelves right behind the register. Customers always checked the food shelves before paying for their purchases. During the holiday season, the popular Patience Brewster's reindeers were moved to the front and sold very well. Jennifer noticed that Baccarat was in high demand. She placed a case of Baccarat products facing the front entrance. The products in that case had to be constantly replenished that year. During the holiday season, international tourists often asked for Christofle and Baccarat. We had very few Christofle products. They bought Baccarat.

Jennifer liked to make her own decisions and she didn't seem to like the way her manager David tried to control her. He was probably worried about the success of Gift Gallery, as a major managerial change had just taken place. Therefore, he had a tendency to micromanage her. If Jennifer was absent, David came to our department, walked around, checked everything, and on one occasion, he even reorganized the display of frames. The following day, Jennifer saw the new frame display and changed it completely.

As time passed, she learned and knew more about the inner workings of Gift Gallery than he did. David contributed to the organization of a designer event, endorsing one of the least sold designers in our department. Her products had been on the shelves for years without selling well. We all wondered why Neiman Marcus didn't remove this designer from the store, as her products occupied space that could have been given to better sellers. Her products were made of hammered metal. They were very plain and couldn't compete with the sophisticated and very popular metal products made by Michael Aram. Jennifer wasn't happy about the upcoming event because she knew that sales of this designer were very low. However, she couldn't say anything because David, her boss, had placed his stamp of approval on this designer. I advertised the upcoming event with my customers, who didn't show up.

Only Mrs. Lawrence came because she liked free gifts and, in all store events, customers received some free gifts. During most of the day, the designer sat at her table surrounded by her artworks with very few visitors. Occasionally, a few walk-ins browsed and made a few purchases. Some of the managers made purchases. Some customers who had come to the store to shop in other areas also checked out her products. The sales weren't very high as in previous designer appearances. After the event, this designer's products continued to be sold at Neiman Marcus. Some of them stayed on display, moved from one shelf to another, year after year. They acquired scratches and dents, becoming damaged. That's how we could finally remove them from the sales floor.

In contrast, the Ardmore African art event had drawn a good crowd. The Michael Aram designer event had been unbelievably successful. All salespersons in the store had invited customers to attend the Aram event. Gift Gallery was packed. The customers wanted to meet Michael Aram in person, talk to him, and buy his products. Aram brought a sensational trunk show to our store. I sold about $12,000 in products, which entitled me to $1,200 of free Aram products as commission. Ten percent was an extraordinarily good commission that made salespersons very happy. We were able to pick objects we liked, but wouldn't have been able to afford. The Aram event was repeated the following year. This time it included Aram's jewelry, which was brought and displayed upstairs. This time my sales were only $8,000 because a new Fine Apparel salesperson rang up some of my invited customers with her number, while I was busy assisting other customers. This problem couldn't be rectified. However, the organization of these designer appearances was superb because Jennifer constantly communicated with Lisa who was extremely experienced in Gift Gallery events.

One morning, as I came to work, I was told to follow Jennifer and David to David's office. Apparently, I was in trouble. I was puzzled because I couldn't think of anything I did wrong. They explained what the problem was: Lenny, a salesperson in the Beauty department, had complained about me. A few days earlier, my favorite perfume had gone on 30/10. That means that I could apply my 30% employee discount on it, plus an additional 10%. We were allowed to make purchases when we were clocked out. Therefore, before clocking in, I had approached Lenny. There were no customers around his counter. He told me that my perfume didn't have an additional 10% off. I wrote a check for the amount he quoted, as employees could only pay with cash or check. He seemed incapable of processing my check. He tried multiple times, unsuccessfully. A Beauty manager walked by. I asked her about the extra 10% discount.

"Yes, your perfume is included in 30/10!" she said.

I wrote a new check and gave it to Lenny, who tried to process my second check also unsuccessfully. It was time for me to clock in. Some customers had started surrounding his register counter. I asked for my check, driver's license, employee card, and perfume.

"I really have to go. I'll have it rung up elsewhere," I told him.

Lenny was quite annoyed by the fact that I was going to purchase the perfume elsewhere in the store. He was going to lose commission. In reality, no one earned commission on my perfume, because I went straight to the Cash Office and asked the two nice ladies who worked there, if they could ring it up. I explained that Lenny didn't seem capable of processing my check and I had run out of time. Brenda and Mariana were amazingly helpful.

"Sure. Just leave everything here. We'll take care of it." And they did. My check was processed without any problem and I purchased my perfume with the correct 30/10 discount.

David and Jennifer told me that Lenny accused me of making a scene in front of the customers and of giving him a bad check. I quickly decided to adopt the self-protection method that I had taught my son when he was in school.

"If anyone attacks you, never react, because if you do, you end up in trouble." This tactic proved golden when my son was physically attacked by a classmate who pushed him against a fence, in front of a crowd of students. My son didn't react at all. Had he fought back, the school would have said that he had engaged in a fight. The other child got in trouble. My son didn't and from then on, no one physically attacked him again.

Now, I was in a similar predicament. Jennifer continued to repeat that I had given a bad check to the company, that I had been very rude to Lenny, and that I had made a scene in front of the customers. I listened and spoke very little. It did have a slightly disarming effect, as she kept repeating the same things without getting any reaction from me. Jennifer and David didn't relent. Jennifer placed a sheet of paper in front of me and asked me to sign it. The paper contained a series of false accusations including the allegation that I had given a bad check to the company. I silently signed this paper because there was no other way to keep my job. That signed document was placed in my file, but I knew that if it ever had a follow-up in the corporate office, I could prove that my check had been processed by Neiman Marcus on that day.

I wasn't happy about this story. I was disappointed with Lenny verbally attacking me. I had always been very nice to him and I had tried to give him a sale that I could have given to any other salesperson in the store. He didn't consider me part of his team. Was he a team player? I could never understand why he was unable to process checks. It was a very unusual episode. The store had a group of very friendly and capable employees. We all got along and helped each other. From then on, I always asked my best friends to ring up my purchases, even if they weren't in the department in which I was making the purchase. I don't know what happened to Lenny. Months later, he was gone.

Another incident caused by improper communication took place in August, when our summer sales started. All products included in the sale had an initial 40% price drop. Since any Neiman Marcus store could pull and sell products present in our store, I immediately tackled Jay Strongwater products because they were quite expensive even on sale and in high demand. On the first day of the sale, I started texting pictures and prices of all the Strongwater sale products to customers interested in this designer, while Jennifer was perfecting the displays.

"Someone wants the horse head," I announced almost immediately. It was a life-size horse head, hand-painted and covered with Swarovski crystals, that cost several thousands of dollars on sale. Jennifer was stunned. She was just starting to find out that I had very powerful customers.

"How about if I get the box and you continue texting," she said. That made me very happy because retrieving boxes wasted sales time. While she was getting the box, I texted Mrs. Lansing, the woman who liked to use her American Express card only. Mrs. Lansing had come into the store a few months earlier. She had seen a large standing Strongwater cheetah in one of the vitrines.

"Let me know when it goes on sale!" she had said before leaving.

However, when she received my text and saw the list of all Strongwater products included in the sale, she noticed the lion clock. She replied, asking for details about it. The lion clock was a phenomenal clock on a marble base with a roaring lion. Mrs.

Lansing liked the fact that some malachite was used to decorate this artwork. I knew that another customer, Mr. Jones, was interested in the lion clock, but he hadn't responded to my text. As the clock was more expensive than the cheetah, I encouraged the purchase and Mrs. Lansing decided to buy it. Later in the day, I got hold of Mr. Jones.

"Are you still interested in the Strongwater lion clock?" I asked him, knowing that there was one still available in another store.

"Yes."

"I sold the one in our store, but I will have the last one shipped to you from another store," I told him.

A few days later, Mr. Jones informed me that the lion clock had been delivered to him with a cracked marble base. The clock had been shipped in the wrong box without sufficient padding. Mrs. Lansing should have bought the cheetah and Mr. Jones should have bought the lion clock, which we had in our store. We had both the original boxes. Had I discouraged the clock and encouraged the cheetah, Mrs. Lansing would have bought the cheetah. Unfortunately, I always go for a sure sale and the lion clock was more expensive than the cheetah.

Mr. Jones indicated that he wanted the clock repaired because he loved it. I told him that repairs usually took six to eight weeks. He brought the clock into the store and Jennifer contacted the Strongwater company. Eight weeks turned into three months, and then into six months.

"He can return the lion clock and get a full refund," she kept repeating. Mr. Jones liked the clock and didn't want to return it.

"I sent them an email, but they didn't respond," Jennifer kept telling me. I don't know why she couldn't pick up the phone to tackle the problem. At last, the Strongwater company replied.

"They are waiting for the right type of marble to arrive from Italy," she reported. About twelve months after the delivery of the broken clock, Mr. Jones was furious because he had paid thousands of dollars and there wasn't a realistic deadline for the repair. He had been a very devoted Strongwater collector, but stopped making purchases.

"They informed me that they were unable to get the same marble from Italy," Jennifer found out.

"Can't they use a different type of marble?" I asked.

Jennifer hadn't thought about that. She asked and finally they replaced the cracked black marble base with a gray marble base. This could have been done six months earlier. Mr. Jones was very happy with the repair, but it came too late. I had lost a very loyal customer. Slow and ineffective communication had suppressed Mr. Jones' passion for Strongwater products. He no longer trusted me nor our store.

A third unfortunate occurrence, caused by lack of communication, took place during a Neiman Marcus store event. A couple of customers, Mr. and Mrs. Redding, came into our department to make some purchases and fell in love with the large Mackenzie Childs Merrifield chandelier, hanging from the ceiling. It had colorful ceramic birds holding the lights. It cost about $7,000. As the couple had specific questions about the purchase and possible installation of the chandelier, I had to get Jennifer involved. She said that we had to sell the chandelier present in our store, meaning a used one, and that we couldn't install it. However, as Jennifer suggested, we had an "In Circle" event coming up in a month and the chandelier was going to be included. During "In Circle," customers could use their Neiman Marcus store card and get a large number of points. I continued to communicate with the potential buyers. Mrs. Redding was going to be in Europe during this event, but she was interested in buying the chandelier. She insisted that she wanted a new chandelier from the warehouse. With some negotiation, I convinced Jennifer to allow a new chandelier. This purchase was going to be a special order. I reminded the customer that special orders couldn't be cancelled.

"What if the lamp is delivered with a problem?" she asked.

"Then we can replace it, but we can't cancel it."

On the first day of the event, Mrs. Redding called from Europe and told me that she wanted to speak directly with the manager before making her purchase. She wanted the manager to confirm that the chandelier was going to be replaced if it arrived damaged. I asked Jennifer to contact the customer, but she never did. The following day, while I was off, Mrs. Redding called another salesperson she had dealt with in the past. It was Robin, the salesperson who had transferred from our department to the Handbags department when I was hired. Robin rang up the chandelier in the store and took the sale entirely.

When I discovered that the chandelier had been sold by Robin, I complained to Jennifer because I should have received at least half of this sale, since I had been working on it for several weeks. Jennifer spoke with David, who didn't allow the sale to be switched or split. Two weeks later, Mrs. Redding came into our store and asked me where her chandelier was.

"I have no idea. You purchased the chandelier from another salesperson," I told her.

She said that she had asked Robin to ring up the chandelier for me. Apparently, Robin knew I was the salesperson, but she had totally ignored it.

Mrs. Redding had made a terrible mistake: she had contacted a different salesperson and lost me forever. I always removed disloyal customers from my list. I was never going to fight in her favor again. She now had to deal with a salesperson in the Handbags department, which wasn't ideal. Mrs. Redding found out that she was going to receive the chandelier that used to be hanging in our store. It had already been taken down and packed. She was furious because Jennifer and I had promised a new one from the warehouse. It was no longer my problem. It was Jennifer's problem. I heard Jennifer having long phone conversations with

Mrs. Redding, while sitting at her desk in the stockroom. The chandelier sale had taken a wrong direction due to lack of proper communication. I don't know which chandelier the customer ended up with because I completely distanced myself from this transaction.

Betraying a salesperson to purchase from a different one in another department was always an error at Neiman Marcus, if the customer wanted to continue receiving information and wanted to shop well. Regular salespersons didn't just place sales. They worked around the rules protecting the customers' interests and striving to grant their wishes. They acted as knowledgeable advocates who fought for their customers' benefit. I've seen customers get away with outrageous requests simply because they had a good buffer between themselves and the managers.

Some customers kept multiple regular salespersons throughout the store, depending on the department in which they shopped. Other ones relied only on one person, who wasn't always as well informed as the specialist in a specific area. A Russian customer contacted Nadia, a Russian salesperson, to purchase some Mackenzie Childs outdoor furniture on sale. When they arrived together in my department, I explained which items were on sale and I gave Nadia essential information she didn't have. The customer had shopped at Neiman Marcus for a long time. She quickly realized that Nadia didn't have sufficient knowledge of the sale. Although she liked dealing with a salesperson from her home country, she continued to shop with me in my specialty area afterwards. I helped her get some beautiful Mackenzie Childs products that weren't in our store and that I advertised only with my best Mackenzie Childs customers. Had she continued to shop with Nadia in Gift Gallery, she would have missed out.

After the Covid pandemic started in 2020, store traffic slowed down. In March, suddenly and without any previous announcement, the store was closed. Towards the end of the last business day, the managers took money out of all the registers and informed us that we were going to continue selling with our phones at home. No one knew how long the store was going to remain closed, but the company had good plans in place for us. They added a new feature to our phones that allowed us to ring up customers. This feature was supposed to be introduced at a later time, but due to the pandemic store closures, the company decided to make it available immediately. A series of changes occurred. We received special training through zoom calls.

During the store closures, Jennifer was laid off like many other managers. My new manager was Lisa again! She was managing Gift Gallery, in addition to the Fine Jewelry and Fashion Jewelry departments. I was happy to have her back. She was prompt in communicating and always answered all my questions through the phone.

We continued to work at home, clocking in and clocking out with our phones. Our hours were reduced, but Lisa told me that

I could add my unused vacation hours to my reduced schedule, turning it into a regular schedule. I was going to receive the same pay, plus commission on my sales. During my lunch break, I used to take a long walk making multiple loops around my apartment complex, always bringing my phone. Customers were aware of the fact that their favorite store was struggling. Therefore, they were placing a high number of orders. The company offered discounts, particularly in Beauty. Many customers were remodeling and purchasing home decor objects. One of my regular customers decided to replace all her old table lamps since they were discounted. If the time of the pandemic closures was disastrous for many people, shamefully, I have to admit that it was positive for my work. I used to sit comfortably on the couch with my phone to advertise products and place orders. It was nice to be able to sit on the couch while working and not have to hear David reproaching me:

"Why are you leaning against the wall?" "Are you holding the building?" "I just finished talking with a salesperson downstairs who was leaning against the desk and here you're doing the same!" "You have to stand straight! It's not good for the customers to come in and see the salesperson leaning against the wall."

He was absolutely heartless when it came to standing straight. We all had a tendency to lean for a few minutes, but we all worked very hard and placed good sales. The job required a lot of physical exertion. As soon as I started my shift, I had to move large boxes, bend, pull, lift etc.

"My workout for the day has started," I used to say.

When we were just texting or communicating with customers by phone, it was nice to lean against a wall or a desk for a short time. After David caught us, we used to exchange his comments and laugh. I tried to avoid getting caught when he walked by. I was fairly safe when he was in his office. Sometimes, he took a picture of me leaning against the wall and then texted it to me from the opposite side of the floor. It was actually funny, but with David you couldn't laugh too much because he really meant it. The salespersons in the Fine Apparel department, the area he controlled directly, had a luxurious desk and chair that they used to sit on, taking turns. I was so envious of them. I could see them from Gift Gallery, while leaning against the wall. They were much more comfortable than I was, while making money for the company just like I did. The year before the pandemic struck, I caught a terrible cold because the air conditioning vent had an unusually strong blow of air for about a week. Eventually, they fixed the problem. With my cold, I struggled to stand up all day and I was busy! Since at the time we had a table with bar chairs on display, I used to sit for a while on one of the bar chairs while there were no customers. Shelley was aware of my cold and didn't mind. Thankfully, David never caught me. He would have been very mad.

While we worked at home, the Shipping department was open. A few managers took turns working inside the store. We could contact them for any reason. We could ask them to ring up a product that was in the store, using our employee number. I contacted David once to sell a huge Mackenzie Childs frog butler holding a tray. The frog had been returned and was still wrapped in the Shipping department. The first buyer loved it, but when it was delivered to his house, he discovered that his wife didn't like frogs. I had no trouble finding a second buyer because the frog butler was useful and funny. David rang up the purchase on a register in the store, with my number.

Lisa monitored all her salespersons' sales. At the end of each day, we had to communicate to her the amount of our total sales and she always replied with a positive comment. Employees who didn't have significant sales were laid off.

Our store reopened in May, just when I had finished adding all my extra vacation hours. I never lost any money during the store closure. We reopened in steps: first only by appointment and with many cautionary procedures. I was in the first group that returned to the store. It was a skeletal staff, but very motivated to make money for the company.

We had lots of training sessions ahead. The company continued to add features to our phones allowing us to create and email a visual set of matching products to advertise and sell. We were taught how to send group emails and how to reach customers in the most effective way. The company also required mandatory email contacts, assigning a list of leads to all salespersons each week. No one liked the new mandatory emailing system. Most salespersons, including myself, preferred to text customers, in order to reach them quickly. With texts, I usually received immediate response and instantaneous sales. It was a very effective method of communication. However, since I had to adhere to company requirements, each week I emailed my 50-60 leads as fast as I could, to get them out of the way. Other salespersons told me that they also tried to get their mandatory leads quickly out of the way, in order to concentrate on their real sales. Most leads were unknown customers with whom we hadn't established any business connection. In my mandatory list, I would also find some regular customers. I usually texted these customers using my established method of communication because I didn't want to jeopardize my chances of getting sales from them. My texts or emails weren't as fancy as the corporate office would have liked them to be, but my sales were so high that no one above me ever complained. As long as we succeeded in selling, our managers didn't care about the way we contacted our regular customers.

I also emailed some sets of matching products according to the procedures we learned during special training sessions. I never obtained any sales that way because the system was too predictable and generic. Instead, I used a unique and unpredictable method of communication to keep my customers' attention. I used a lot of humor, which the customers seemed to enjoy. For example, if I was advertising some hot sauces, for the hottest one I would add in my description, "...and if you like hell in a bottle..." Customers loved the humor and mentioned it when they texted me back to place their orders. They always read my texts because they were curious to see what I was sending. My messages always contained pictures, precise dimensions, and accurate descriptions of products that I typed myself. I rarely used pre-printed online information because the personalized method seemed to be more effective. I wanted the customers to feel like they were communicating with me and not just reading information available on the website.

I searched online and identified unusual products appropriate for the season, such as motorized pool floats in the summer. Sometimes, I combined products that we had in the store with other ones of the same nature available in the warehouse. These were personalized choices that I made for my audience. I texted constantly, fearing many times that my customers would get tired of receiving my messages. Surprisingly, customers used to express their positive reaction.

"Please, keep sending pictures and new products!" "I have you in my phone contacts. I love your texts!" "I always check all your texts."

If they had questions, they responded immediately.

"What was the size of the fifth one?" "Do you have seven of them?" "Is the second one still available?" Customer communication was non-stop.

For major holidays, I always sent my best wishes using a humorous vignette appropriate for the occasion. Customers laughed and texted back. One year, around Easter time, I found a stunning picture of a basket filled with hand-painted "Wendish" eggs. I sent that picture with my best wishes for the spring season. I was bombarded by messages asking me how much the eggs cost. Customers thought I was selling them. Sadly, I had to reply that I was only sending my best wishes. Those eggs would have sold so well! Neiman Marcus customers did appreciate art and responded well to anything artistic. It should have been obvious that I wasn't selling those Wendish eggs because I hadn't indicated the price nor the size and I hadn't described the decorating technique, which I would have done if the products were for sale. And yet, customers still replied to my text asking to buy those eggs. I continued to use my system, which reflected my personality, obtaining good results.

Years of texting always taught me something new. As I texted a series of tech accessories on sale, unexpectedly I learned that they sold instantly. These types of products weren't brand related. They elicited immediate positive response. This means that I could sell them to a Baccarat customer and to a Mackenzie Childs customer. David used to complain that I sold too many products on sale.

"Why don't you focus on full price products?" he often asked me.

I did focus on them and I even sold multiple full price Moncler coats in his department. Yet, I never lost sight of the sale products because they made up a large number of add-ons to my sales. Customers loved them because they knew they were acquiring a product that was almost sold out or difficult to catch. Mackenzie Childs customers were thrilled to be able to buy a Christmas wreath in their favorite brand, at a fraction of the price.

"If I sold only products on sale, I wouldn't be able to reach my goals," was my reply to him. It was true. Those products alone wouldn't have been sufficient to reach the high goals given to me by the company.

"Don't listen to David!" my third manager Natalie used to say. "Keep doing what you're doing."

I did. I continued to sell full price products and products on sale. If I had focused only on full price products, I also would have spoiled the surprise factor of my texts. Customers never knew what they were going to receive and they loved that.

"Keep sending!" was their reaction.

8

Change It Up!

All companies go through constant changes. They introduce improvements and adjustments adapting to new economic factors that affect their business, dealing with customers' new ways of shopping, simplifying or updating their technology, and strengthening their identity. Changes are continuous and often hardly detectable by the common shopper. A business can start failing when its system is no longer right for the changed circumstances in which it operates. Companies that don't recognize the signs of their failure usually continue to apply the same procedures until it's too late to make a change. Companies that are able to recover are particularly prone to introducing many infrastructural changes that guarantee their survival and success. Like all companies, Neiman Marcus was subjected to the Covid pandemic blow, which required immediate changes in order to help customers shop. Additionally, after emerging from Chapter 11, the company adopted a complete reorganization, from the corporate office to the individual stores.

From the onset of the Covid pandemic, we were bombarded by a series of operational modifications. During the store closure, we were given a phone feature that allowed us to ring up customers. When the store reopened, the introduction of "Shop by appointment" was a true game changer. It allowed the group of salespersons back in the store to become comfortable selling in all departments. The managers wrote our names on a list indicating our turn to help incoming customers. As we finished assisting a customer, our name was placed at the bottom of the list. While we were waiting for our next turn, we could text and place sales with our phone. If we were really busy placing orders with the phone, we could skip our turn and let the next person in line take our place.

Many Covid cautionary procedures were implemented. All clothes tried on by the customers were steamed. This was a little problematic because sometimes the only size available couldn't be tried on or sold, as it was waiting to be steamed. We kept a distance of six feet from the customers, even on the escalator. Customers were supposed to be in front of us and we were several steps behind. We wore masks which were extremely annoying. It was difficult to understand when customers were speaking. If I was far away from everyone else, I lowered my mask just to catch a good breath of air. If I was very close to a customer, I actually used to hold my breath behind the mask as an additional precaution. Neiman Marcus provided free disposable masks for salespersons and for customers who showed up without a mask. After trying many different types of masks, the best ones for me turned out to be silk Slip masks, sold at Neiman Marcus. They were shiny and beautiful. They came in different colors and they were breathable. Many employees and even some managers started wearing these Slip masks.

During "Shop by appointment," business was very fast because customers showed up at the store and lined up outside the front entrance, in spite of the Covid outbreak. Customers were allowed inside the store one at a time (or one group at a time) as a salesperson became available.

"I need to shop in the Men's Shoe department," a customer would announce entering the store. The salesperson took the customer to the Shoe department and without any previous training in that area started the sale. After assisting a few customers, we quickly learned what was on the sales floor and where to find the shoes in the multiple Men's Shoes stockrooms. I winged it in Men's Shoes, Women's Shoes, Men's Jewelry, Women's Cosmetics, Men's Perfumes and so forth. I winged it everywhere, learning how to sell in all departments. Generally, the managers tried to assign customers to a specialist, but business was moving fast and everyone was busy somewhere in the store, as only a small group of employees was present. Baccarat seemed to follow me even in Beauty. I sold a very high number of Baccarat perfumes due to luck. The customer just asked for multiple bottles of Baccarat perfumes. Initially, I didn't even know where they were kept. The large sale entitled me to a free Baccarat perfume bottle as commission, which I never took because I prefer my own perfume.

Multi-tasking became even more critical during this phase of sales. While assisting a customer in one area, we had to quickly go to another department to retrieve a product requested by phone and make sure it didn't sell out. As I was helping a man in the Men's Jewelry department one day, I received a texted request for a YSL handbag.

"I will be with you ASAP. Finishing with a customer," was my typical reply, to give myself some time. After picking his necklace, this young man started choosing clothes. He said he needed all these products to go out, now that restaurants and bars were reopening in Florida. As soon as I was able to send him into a fitting room, I raced to Loss Prevention to get a key to the Handbags cases. Then, I went to grab the requested YSL handbag and returned the key I had checked out.

"I have your bag. I'll ring it up as soon as I can," was my reassuring text to the pending customer. The customers waited graciously. They knew that their orders were going to be fulfilled.

When the young man came out of the fitting room, I was holding in my hands the clothes and jewelry he had picked.

"I'm not buying that handbag," he said, noticing that I had the bag on top of his clothes.

"I know. It's for another customer," I told him with a smile.

These customers had no idea of the extent of multi-tasking and multi-selling we engaged in. They thought that we were taking care of one customer at a time.

"Shop by appointment" lengthened my list of regular customers. As I was helping a small group of ladies from out of town in the Women's Shoes area, these ladies tried on and purchased multiple pairs of shoes.

"When are the Louboutin shoes going on sale?" they asked me before leaving. I had to check with the area manager. The sale was going to start a couple of weeks later.

"Don't worry, I'll text you as soon as the sale starts," I told them.

Two weeks later, I took pictures of all the shoes on sale, including the Louboutin brand, and started texting my out-of-town customers plus other customers who had never bought shoes from me before. Trying to sell shoes by phone during a sale is a full-time job in itself, as I quickly learned. I was inundated with requests. Customers sent me a picture of the shoes they were interested in and asked for details.

"Do you have this one in size 6?" "Do you have this one in black?" "Do you have these sandals in size 7 or 7.5?" I had so many shoes to search, pull, ring up, and take to Shipping that I had to step out of the "Shop by appointment" for a while. If the shoes that the customer wanted weren't available in the correct size or color, I tried to find a similar style or the same style in a different color. It was an immense amount of work. Eventually, I returned to the front of the store with my stack of receipts to turn in to the manager and get my name back in the "Shop by appointment" list. Managers didn't like it when salespersons disappeared.

"Where did you go? You were next in line 45 minutes ago."

"I was selling shoes." Then, I handed in my receipts, which appeased the manager very quickly.

"Shop by appointment" lasted several weeks. Other groups of salespersons started arriving and populating the various departments of the store. The managers asked us to go back to our specialty areas and introduced new territorial rules. We could now assist any customer we saw without a salesperson, even in a different department. However, we weren't allowed to stand outside our specialty area waiting for a customer.

Gift Gallery was surrounded by multiple clothing areas, Lingerie, and Children's.

If I wasn't busy with a customer in my area, I kept my eyes open and immediately ran to a customer without help anywhere around me. Sometimes, I checked the merchandise displayed in other areas surrounding Gift Gallery, and I was able to catch a browsing customer that way. I was still careful not to cross others' territories.

"Is someone helping you" or "Are you helping him?" were typical questions in case of uncertainty. Loyal customers announced their arrival by phone and clearly indicated who was helping them, if asked. After placing a customer in the fitting room, if I saw a customer in Gift Gallery from the opposite side of the floor, I ran back to my area to get that sale as well. Leaning against the wall had become a thing of the past. We were all ready to take customers anywhere around us. I had to be watchful because Clothing salespersons could now sell in Gift Gallery or in Children's if nobody was there. If multiple customers entered the Children's department, the manager used to alert all salespersons with her phone.

"All available salespersons go to Children's!"

This new system increased everyone's volume of sales. Everyone was really busy and no one cared if someone from another department made a sale in his or her specialty area because that's what everyone did. I no longer had downtime.

While Lisa was still my manager, I told her that we had very few Baccarat products, which had been placed on a low shelf in the back. She contacted the vendor who promptly showed up. I don't think that the Baccarat representatives were happy with the way the few pieces we had were displayed in the store, although they didn't say anything. More Baccarat products started arriving, but not as many as we used to have. The company had come out of Chapter 11, was restructuring, and didn't seem to stock as abundantly as it used to. I had to use my phone to find pieces available elsewhere. When a Baccarat sale started, I texted my Baccarat customers immediately because most products were usually sold out within 24 hours. On one occasion, I contacted a physician who loved to collect Baccarat glasses and decanters. He placed an order for a small number of wine glasses. As soon as he received them, he asked me for more. They were all sold out everywhere. He was very upset. He said that he had been busy visiting patients, but he should have placed a larger order.

I was spending a large amount of time selling in the Children's department. Traffic was high in that area, as the company had added many new designer brands. The Children's department continued to take space away from Gift Gallery. One of the Children's department salespersons was Gillian, who had replaced Sara months earlier. She asked Julie to split sales with her in the Children's department, but Julie refused. I don't know how Gillian made money because before the 2020 election, she used her downtime to handwrite postcards to voters, instead of texting customers. The managers never caught her and I minded my own business. I thought she was cutting her income even if she didn't get reprimanded. The general manager called her into her office once because her outfits weren't adequate for Neiman Marcus. She was asked to step up her clothes.

One morning, while neither Julie nor Gillian were there, I was working in the Children's department, which had intense traffic. I helped a customer who requested to have her purchases rung up for Julie, who was at home with her husband and son, infected with Covid. She couldn't sell in the store until her family members tested negative. We always rang up purchases for another salesperson if the customer requested it. It meant satisfying customer loyalty. The salesperson assisting the customer technically had the right to take half of the sale. I never did and many other salespersons didn't. I helped the customer pick the children's clothes and as I was about to ring them up, Gillian appeared out of nowhere saying that Lisa had sent her to ring up the purchase. I told her that the customer wanted to have the purchase rung up for Julie. However, Gillian took the entire sale for herself. After the customer left, I reminded Gillian that the customer had requested to have the sale rung up for Julie and that she had been disgraceful to take it. I complained to Lisa. Gillian also complained to Lisa because I had called her "disgraceful." Julie had called Lisa to alert her that one of her customers was making a purchase. Lisa didn't know that I was in the Children's department assisting this customer. Gillian apparently had arrived in the store and Lisa had asked her to assist the customer. Now, both Gillian and I were standing in front of Lisa, in her office.

"We don't call each other names," Lisa said looking at me, "although we may think of these names in our mind," she continued looking at her. She didn't really get mad at either of us and she didn't say if she was going to fix the sale. Neiman Marcus managers never seemed to get involved in sales disputes. As I had worked with Julie for years and we were friends, I decided to take action because this sale shouldn't have been taken away from someone who was at home due to the fact that her husband and son were infected with Covid. Julie was really upset when I told her what had happened.

"Don't worry! I'll get your sale back," I promised her.

The following day, I went directly to the HR office and spoke with Audrey, the employee who could formalize a split or switched sale. I think that Lisa had already alerted her, but the sale was still in Gillian's name. I explained what happened.

"Are you sure you don't want half of the sale?" Audrey asked me, since I was entitled to it.

"No, because the customer specifically asked to have the sale rung up for Julie and because I would never do that to Julie in her present condition," I said.

Audrey nodded. She had a husband, too. She understood. Everyone was very concerned about the spreading of the disease and the havoc it was causing to families. We all worked and prayed not to get sick. Audrey switched the sale to Julie. Gillian didn't last very long in our store. She was laid off with other employees and managers.

Barbara was hired in the Children's department to replace Gillian. She frequently used to go to text in the stockroom using her personal phone. She wasn't texting Neiman Marcus customers. Julie and I thought she had another job on the side, but we could never confirm that. What we quickly learned was that Barbara couldn't count. She had been assigned to a department that received thousands of dollars in cash. At the end of each day, she had to count the money in her register and bring the amount in excess to the cash office. Every time I counted the Children's register, if I was the first employee in the department, the register had too much or too little money. The register couldn't be opened until the cash office checked how much money had been turned in the night before against the register closing slip, so that the money could be adjusted. Additionally, the register count itself was frequently off. All employees on the second floor realized that it was dangerous to use the Children's register because if the amount was off, anyone who had shared that register was under scrutiny. The employees in Clothing areas started to ring up Children's customers in their areas. I decided to start using the Gift Gallery register for Children's purchases. One day when I was covering Barbara's lunch hour, each time I had a sale, I told the customers to follow me to the Gift Gallery register.

"The Children's register was offline earlier. Let's go this way," and the customers followed me, without any problem.

The following day, there was a large shortage in the Children's register. The only employee who had been on that register was Barbara. I told Brenda and Mariana how I had channeled all Children's customers to my Gift Gallery register. They laughed, but they knew that I had made a safe choice because now I wasn't in any way connected to the shortage. I don't think that Barbara was taking money. I really believe that she couldn't count and all the salespersons on the second floor were talking about it. She was never laid off. One day, she just didn't come to work. At first, we heard that her father was ill. Then, we heard that she was ill. It may have been true because she used to tell me that she needed to run to the pharmacy to pick up her prescriptions during her lunch hour. She never came back.

Since the number of our managers continued to decrease, the remaining managers had to take over multiple departments. One morning, I was told that Lisa was no longer our manager. She was managing multiple departments on the first floor. Gift Gallery and the Children's department were assigned to Natalie, who already controlled multiple clothing areas on the second floor. I always thought that assigning Children's to a clothing manager made sense because we sold primarily children's designer clothes. However, Gift Gallery could have been left with the Jewelry manager because many of our products had Swarovski crystals, precious, and semi-precious materials. The store was reorganizing its human resources, based on other criteria.

Both Julie and I were very sad to lose Lisa for the second time. We had both been hired by Lisa and had tremendous respect for her. Our new manager Natalie was a very experienced manager, who seemed to have very little knowledge of and interest in Gift Gallery. Her office was in one of the clothing areas. She rarely walked to my department to check what was happening. Since she was very busy, she hired an assistant named Leyla, who seemed even less interested than her in Gift Gallery.

Leyla took over most of the stocking. Although many shelves in the stockroom were labeled with brand names, she started placing products of the same brand on different shelves, totally disregarding labels. Suddenly, large books appeared downstairs among the Mackenzie Childs products, which were already very copious and didn't need to lose any shelf space. I asked Leyla why she wasn't putting books in the book area upstairs.

"They are too heavy. I can't take them upstairs," she said.

None of us was particularly strong, but we all managed to carry books upstairs or downstairs, except for the stocking person. When she carried light books upstairs, she didn't place them in the book area only. She left them wherever she could find an empty spot. Michael Aram's products were divided by collection. This was very important because there were multiple Aram collections and new ones were constantly being added. Salespersons had to be quick in identifying a product to be sold. Leyla was mixing the collections. I had to check all the collections to find a specific product. Some Children's frames were now mixed with Aram frames upstairs, although they had always been stocked in the Children's stockroom area, downstairs.

When opening boxes, the stocker traditionally kept only boxes of collectors' items or boxes of important designers, to be given to the customers making purchases. Leyla started throwing all kinds of boxes in the empty space surrounded by the stockroom flights of stairs. She threw into this vertical space useless cardboard boxes that should have been discarded and boxes of precious collector's items. Some Michael Aram boxes were also there, although Aram boxes were traditionally kept in the Box Room, where shelves were labeled with the names of his different collections. Needless to say, no one could easily find Aram boxes anymore. Salespersons from other departments placing sales in Gift Gallery were particularly challenged. I had the advantage of knowing the shape of many product boxes. Many Jay Strongwater boxes were now mixed with Michael Aram boxes, meaning that they were almost impossible to find. This was a problematic situation because Strongwater products required the original box with appropriate padding to protect the crystals. No one would have bought an expensive Strongwater product without its original box. One morning, as I started my shift, David asked me to help find the box for a Strongwater elephant figurine that Julie was supposed to ring up. I was able to identify the box in the middle of Aram's boxes.

If I recognized a box that I needed in the space between the stairs, I would call an employee in the Shipping department to retrieve it because I couldn't climb over the railing with a dress or tight skirt, besides the fact that I had no intention of fracturing more bones. The Shipping employees had to acrobatically climb the railing, search through the messy pile of boxes, and climb over the railing again after finding the right box. It wasn't safe. Eventually, the pile of boxes grew so high that no one could search for a specific box.

The mountain of boxes between the flights of stairs also seemed to have become a fire hazard.

The entire store was talking about our stockroom mess, but Natalie didn't seem to notice. Whenever I approached her to communicate a problem, her answer was invariably the same.

"I'm sorry, but I'm very busy now. I will look into it." If I couldn't find a box or a product, I called her, but she was always too busy to come to Gift Gallery.

"Call Leyla! She'll help you find it," was the extent of Natalie's help. Leyla came to Gift Gallery, spent several minutes trying to understand what she had to look for, searched everywhere, and never found anything. She had no idea of where she put things. I learned to bypass both Natalie and Leyla. In the Box Room, if I saw boxes of products that we no longer carried in the store, I threw them in the trash can. However, I didn't have much time to look for boxes to be trashed. Time truly translated into money for salespersons. Stocking wasn't my responsibility. The only person who occasionally tried to improve the situation was James. In his spare time, he used to go to the Box Room and reorganize the shelves as much as he could. It didn't last long. Since the products on the shelves were often in the wrong place, salespersons from other departments became very careless. They threw boxes in the wrong places while they were searching. Some boxes were thrown on the floor. Poor James couldn't keep up with the mess, because it was truly a problem to be addressed by a manager. Many employees throughout the store told Lisa that the Gift Gallery stockroom was out of control. Occasionally, Lisa came to our floor and took a look around. There was nothing she could do because Gift Gallery was no longer her department.

The chaotic situation reached its apex right before a "Gift with purchase" event in Gift Gallery. Customers spending a specific amount of money could choose one of multiple gifts by major designers, such as Jay Strongwater, Michael Aram, Mackenzie Childs, Aerin, and Juliska. The gifts were available until supplies lasted. It was usually a very successful event. Regular customers placed holds on products to be purchased and on their gift to make sure they received it. The gifts used to arrive in our store about seven to ten days before the event started. I used to send pictures of the gifts to my customers, so that they could place their holds. Some customers preferred to physically come into the store to see the gift selection. That year, a couple of gifts arrived 10 days prior to the event and James brought them to our department. I waited for the other gifts to arrive, in order to text all the pictures at the same time. A week later, there was still no trace of the rest of the gifts. I asked James.

"They all came in," he said.

"Where did you put them?"

"I left them on the manager's desk with the other ones," said James.

"They aren't there!"

"Ask Leyla. She probably moved them," he said.

I asked Leyla.

"I didn't see them. They didn't arrive," she claimed.

"Leyla said that the gifts haven't arrived," I told James.

"I brought them to Gift Gallery. They are in the store all right!" he said.

I approached Natalie. She was totally uncooperative.

"I'm really busy now. I'm sure the gifts will arrive," was her flat answer.

She didn't understand that these gifts guaranteed sales. She was used to managing clothing areas where customers showed up in person during a "Purchase with gift" event. Many of my customers lived out of town or out of state. They placed holds and made purchases without coming into the store. They didn't receive any pictures in advance that year. I announced the upcoming event, apologizing for the fact that the gifts weren't in our store yet. I had no holds. The day before the event started, Natalie realized that the gifts were still missing, except for a couple of them that had arrived early. James told her that all gifts had arrived more than a week earlier. Natalie confronted Leyla, who finally admitted that she had taken them and moved them elsewhere, although she had told me that she had never even seen them. The gifts were retrieved. Leyla lost her assistant role in our department. She was sent to the first floor to work for other departments.

It was a major relief to get rid of her because within a few weeks she had caused much havoc. James continued to stock our area, alternating with other Shipping employees. He was able to fix some problems, such as taking books out of the crowded Mackenzie Childs stocking area or combining products of the same brand on the same shelf.

The company continued to send us new Children's brands. The Children's department was increasing in size. New Children's products continued to take over the Gift Gallery shelves, whereas Gift Gallery products were no longer all displayed. They were kept in the stockroom. I used to inspect the stockroom to find something new to advertise to my customers by phone. Some Gift Gallery products were displayed in other parts of the store. On more than one occasion, I couldn't find a product present in the store because it was placed outside of my area. Gradually, the Children's products started taking over the stockroom also. During the holiday season, some Gift Gallery products were stocked in several fitting rooms.

The Children's shoes were spread out everywhere in the stockroom. Some shoe boxes were piled up on the floor. Some of them were on very high shelves that most salespersons couldn't reach even with a ladder. Styles were mixed together. Sometimes, I looked for a shoe size that wasn't on the sales floor and the box in the stockroom was empty. I used to place all the empty boxes on the manager's old desk hoping that Natalie would see them, on the rare occasions when she entered the stockroom. Occasionally, the box in the stockroom contained only one shoe and the other one materialized weeks later in a drawer, mixed with other articles. Some shoes were lost forever. Shoes matching the shoes on display were also frequently missing in the stockroom, which continued to become more and more chaotic. Jennifer would have been horrified if she had seen that mess. She was very precise with regards to organizing shoes.

We lost sales. We could ship products from other locations, but some customers came into the store because they needed the shoes urgently for a child's event. International tourists didn't want a shipment. Shoes stocked in drawers on the sales floor were no longer divided clearly by style. One had to open all drawers to search for a specific shoe style. When one finally learned where it was, the shoes were moved to different drawers. Some Children's clothes were placed in the Michael Aram room. Many blankets and toys sold at low prices were also replacing Aram's more expensive and well-selling products. Mackenzie Childs was moved to the back. Many customers thought that we had stopped selling this brand. Strongwater was in the back. The Strongwater products that used to be in the front vitrine had been replaced with items that didn't have the same high demand. Jan Barboglio's plain metal and glass products were placed in the Strongwater front vitrine. Some customers were intrigued by Jan Barboglio's rustic style. However, the magic sparkle of Strongwater's products, decorated with Swarovski crystals, had a mesmerizing effect on a larger number of customers.

My phone continued to be my true money-making tool in Gift Gallery. On the side, I added sales in other departments. I assisted a customer by phone who ordered for her daughter's wedding 12 Juliska chargers, dinner plates, salad plates, bowls, plus serving trays, serving bowls, tureen, gravy boat, and many more products available in the same collection. Most products were shipped from the warehouse or from other stores. As I tracked the shipments daily, I discovered that the new tracking system on the phone was faulty. It had been very accurate for many years. The phone now indicated the incorrect number of items present in one shipment or the incorrect number of shipments made or the incorrect delivery of items that hadn't been delivered yet. The Shipping department was aware of this problem. Since I was tracking a large number of products, I started using the register to track my shipments because the register was always accurate. If I wasn't in the store, I called the Shipping department and asked someone to track a shipment for me on the register, as I could no longer do it accurately on my phone.

My sales continued to grow thanks to the high number of loyal customers I had built over a period of many years and thanks to my proactive attitude. I was contacting customers continuously. What Gift Gallery needed was a manager who had the time to devote to the department, now left to its own fate.

After my first three years with the company, I was invited to an award lunch at Brio restaurant organized for salespersons who had opened a high number of credit card accounts. At the time, I probably had about $300,000 in sales. When I reached $500,000 in sales, I was invited to an award luncheon at the Capital Grille, which was delicious and fun. We attended this lunch in a private room with David and the general manager. While walking to the Capital Grille, one of my coworkers and I started talking about the famous dinner award open only to top salespersons, which was usually held in a very expensive Orlando restaurant. The dinner required a minimum of $750,000 in sales, although some of the top salespersons sold much more than that.

"I would love to attend this dinner award," I said.

"I think I can make it," my coworker replied. She had transferred from Women's High Apparel to the Men's department, which was extremely lucrative.

"I think I can make it, too," I said, as I had very high sales and enough time to reach the needed amount before the end of the fiscal year.

We both gave each other a high five and promised to meet at the award dinner the following year. Month after month, I kept checking my sales and smiling because I knew I had a chance to attend that coveted dinner party.

Barbara and I had our first performance review with Leyla because Natalie was too busy to take care of it. Leyla read the numbers in my performance sheet and wrote notes on it. At the end of my review, she told me what she expected from me, although she wasn't my manager. I walked out of Natalie's office, where the review had taken place, feeling sad. Barbara said that Leyla had written notes on her review sheet also. She said that Leyla hadn't even been working in our store during the period that she was reviewing for both of us. I'm not sure if she was right, but I realized that we had no manager taking care of us. After Leyla lost her assistant position in Gift Gallery and Children's, Natalie started reviewing me herself. Gradually, when I asked her a question, instead of dismissing me with "I'm sorry, I'm very busy right now," she actually started listening. I think she finally realized that my sales were in excess of goals, which was good for her as a manager.

Julie started feeling pain in her knees. She could no longer stand in the store. After a series of injection treatments to alleviate her pain, she resigned. Barbara vanished and we never found out what exactly had happened to her. Natalie hired a new salesperson in the Children's department, Emily. Unlike Barbara, Emily could count. Although none of us took breaks (except for the mandatory lunch break) in order to maximize our sales, Emily took breaks in the stockroom every so often. It was probably a good idea to sit on a chair and rest for a few minutes, but she didn't have a high sales goal like I did. I had no time for breaks in the stockroom, where I would have missed browsers.

Emily was unaware of many department procedures. If she had to place a hold, she placed the garment in a drawer without a tag that should have indicated the name of the customer, the phone number of the customer, and the date of the hold. Occasionally, she placed an item on hold among the clothes of a different brand. Holds were supposed to be placed on a specific hold shelf with the appropriate hold tag. I tried to explain to her the procedure to be followed for holds, but she never listened to me. She thought it was much faster to throw a piece of clothing in a drawer or to hang it in the wrong area, where no one else could find it and sell it. Both Lisa and Jennifer used to monitor everything in the stockroom, including holds. They knew where everything was on the sales floor and had excellent memory. Under their management, Emily would have known and followed correct procedures.

We used to have a special shelf for store transfers labeled "Option 7." Now that the shelf was occupied by empty boxes and some products, the Shipping employees always struggled to find the "Option 7" products. I started bringing them directly to the Shipping department, although I didn't always have time to do so.

Shipping employees also struggled to find products that people purchased online. They used to come to Gift Gallery and show me a picture of the product.

"Do you know where this is?" they asked.

The "Option 7" method of retrieving products from another store had also been changed after the store had reopened. In the past, if I was trying to sell a product available in another store, I had to call that store to verify how many pieces were actually present. If the product was truly available, I asked the employee in the other store to do an "Option 7," which allowed me to ring up a product that was set aside for me. The other employee tagged the product with the name of the customer, my employee number, and his/her employee number. Then, the tagged product would be placed on the "Option 7" shelf of that store and I could ring up the sale.

Following the lockdown, when the store reopened, I could no longer get hold of a department employee in another store easily. Most of the time, no one answered the phone. After multiple rings, an operator answered, took my phone number, and promised to have an employee from the specific department call me back. They rarely called back. We learned quickly that selling a product that was present in low amounts in other stores had become very difficult, if not impossible. Previously, if there was only one item still present in another store, I was always able to sell it with ease. Now, we could easily sell only products that were in the warehouse or that were present in large quantities in other stores. Like many salespersons, I started exchanging phone numbers with employees in other stores, whenever I happened to talk to one of them. We promised to call each other directly if we needed to do an "Option 7." It was the only way to bypass the operator system. This method still didn't work very well.

In 2021, the company introduced corporate gifts with an enticing discount for large orders. I placed two corporate orders establishing customers for corporate orders in the following years. The company did charge one customer incorrectly for the wrong number of gifts, but I was able to have the mistake corrected quickly. Aside from the mistake that upset the customer, the introduction of corporate gifts with a discount for a large order was a very good novelty. Year after year, I was going to be able to widen this slice of my sales and add more corporate customers to my list of regular customers.

Christmas was difficult during my last couple of years at Neiman Marcus. Gift Gallery products had to be displayed in various parts of the store. Holiday foods were inside our department, outside our department on the same floor, downstairs near the front entrance, downstairs inside the Handbags department, and downstairs between Handbags and Jewelry. In the past, customers used to come to Gift Gallery to buy all their food gifts. Having these foods inside and outside of our department was fine, but having them also in several other places on the first floor made food sales complicated. Customers refused to go downstairs even if I offered to accompany them. Therefore, I went, while they waited in Gift Gallery. I carried multiple bottles and boxes of holiday food items, trying to hold as much as possible in one trip because even the most patient customer wasn't going to wait for me to return downstairs a second time.

Some precious Jay Strongwater frames were now casually placed around the escalator among ornaments or Christmas bells or other products of much lower value. Customers looking for Strongwater frames didn't always see them among lower value products. The expensive frames, of course, weren't safe either. Regardless of brand or value, everything was mixed together outside of Gift Gallery, to entice the customer walking through the store. The overall results must have been good because the store continued with this system. Some Jay Strongwater products were also displayed in locked cases in the Jewelry department. Customers came to look for me in Gift Gallery, asking if I could show them these products. They didn't ask the Jewelry employee because they didn't like the fact that Strongwater products were outside of Gift Gallery. As they complained about it, I tried to reassure them.

"It must be just a temporary display."

Many holiday products, such as Santas Clauses and decorated trees, were now in the narrow hallways around the escalator. It was inconvenient for customers to pick their ornaments attached to the trees, while people walked by in the hallways. In the past, decorated trees and other holiday items were placed in the center of a large room. Customers used to spend hours in that room, which was a real money-making triumph of Christmas.

"You don't do Christmas anymore?" many customers asked with sadness, after the new system of spreading products everywhere had been introduced.

Tabletop products formed a category that was much in demand. Customers constantly came in looking for table runners, napkins, and napkin holders, particularly during the holidays. When Lisa had returned to our department as manager for a short time, I asked her if we could have had a Kim Seybert designer event and she thought that it probably would have attracted many customers. Lisa was aware of the importance of tabletop products and used to carefully plan their display. Now, they were placed in a disorganized fashion on a variety of shelves.

Although some of the changes that had been introduced were difficult, I knew that they were necessary because the company was reorganizing to continue to exist successfully and our store was still open. In 2021, Lord & Taylor had closed all its brick-and-mortar stores. Historically, it was a dramatic event. Lord & Taylor was the first department store that opened in the United States in 1826. It was a legendary symbol of American fashion. The final closing of this iconic department store was now symbolic of the dramatic changes taking place within the retail world. I was very lucky to be with Neiman Marcus. I didn't lose a job and my pay was quite good thanks to my commissions.

Covid continued to accompany our daily work. The company allowed us to take off our masks. The plexiglass wall that had been installed to protect the Loss Prevention department was removed. Clothes were no longer steamed after customers tried them on. In 2022, the company required the use of masks again. We also had disinfectants, purifiers, gloves, and free masks for the customers when needed. The vaccine was never made mandatory in the store. Not all employees were vaccinated. Had the vaccine been mandatory, it might have saved the life of an employee who perished during the Covid pandemic. Her coworkers told me that she had refused to take the vaccine, although she had a medical condition. Everyone was shocked by her death. The reality of the pandemic became more evident. It was changing our store in many ways.

James refused to take the vaccine. He said he was afraid of its potentially risky side effects. Apparently, his entire family hadn't been vaccinated. He was terrified by the thought of having a vaccine injection, but he told me that he was also horrified by the fact that the virus killed its victims very quickly.

"When I go home from work, the first thing I do is take a shower in the side of the house opposite from where my family is," he explained to me, as if a shower could remove a virus from his body. He had no understanding of the risk of infection, but he was lucky. His entire family was lucky as no one contracted the virus.

Gradually, I started getting sick inside the store. I didn't contract the Covid infection, but another problem gradually became more and more severe. For months, each time I ended my work shift, I had very painful pimples on the mucous membranes of my mouth: on my palate, on my tongue, on my gums, on my inner cheeks, in my throat. My face swelled up slightly, particularly around my nose and my mouth. I was probably inhaling something that triggered this reaction. I don't know what had changed inside the store, but something new was causing these pathological symptoms. I had worked at this store for almost seven years without any problem. It wasn't a good change. Was a chemical or a disinfecting product making me sick? I don't know.

Each time I had a day off from work, I improved. For a while, I tried to live with this problem. My dentist prescribed chlorhexidine gluconate to rinse my mouth, but it provided no improvement at all. In May 2022, I took a one-week vacation. Amazingly, my mouth almost completely recovered. When I went back to work, after my first shift, I left the store in a terrible state: I had pimples everywhere inside my mouth and swelling on my face. I realized that I could no longer continue to work in this store. It was devastating because I had embraced my job and I was planning to stay at Neiman Marcus as long as I could. My eyes filled with tears. As usual, I was forced to leave a job for reasons outside of my control.

I sent an email to Natalie, David, and the two corporate office representatives working in our location, explaining that I was resigning because I had become terribly allergic to something inside the store. I didn't give a two weeks' notice because I didn't want to continue to be exposed to the cause of my allergy. I couldn't bear the pain and inflammation any longer. There was nothing I could do to resolve this problem. Leaving such a fabulous store for such a horrible reason felt like leaving Lord & Taylor after breaking my kneecap. One day you can walk, run, climb, swim, and the next day you're struggling with crutches just to get down the hall. It was traumatic.

Leaving Neiman Marcus was very difficult. My job wasn't just another accidental low-pay job. It was now part of my life. I had become integrated within the company to which I devoted all my time and efforts. I liked my role, which unfortunately was no longer possible.

I resigned with about $650,000 in sales and still two months to go before the end of the fiscal year. I know I could have made that $750,000 dinner! What was next? I had to look for a job and fast!

In December 2024, Saks acquired Neiman Marcus. The Neiman Marcus corporate office in Dallas was subsequently closed. The inclusion of Neiman Marcus within Saks Global is another indication of the major business restructuring that followed the Covid pandemic. Many American store chains seem to be failing due to overexpansion, change of consumer habits, and debt. They thrive, expand, and implode. No one can predict whether the Neiman Marcus stores will survive in the future because business is constantly evolving. Due to the changes implemented by Saks, Neiman Marcus is already no longer the same company that it used to be. It has retained its name, but it has a different leadership, which impacts all aspects of its day-to-day business.

9

The Way We Shop Matters

How do you mentally process working for a major designer store one day and having to look for a simple hourly job the next day? Neiman Marcus had offered me something much better than low-wage retail employment, but my health came first. With the same realistic determination that all retail workers share, I kept an open mind and checked what was available. My Neiman Marcus pay had been high. Now, it was time to be sensible and seek a job that could pay my bills, without jeopardizing my health. We all sacrifice dreams to pay the bills. One of my coworkers at Walmart told me that he had two jobs when he started working in our store. He also worked as a salesperson at Lowe's. A year later, he had three jobs. Once a week, he worked as a maintenance person in a third company.

"Do you ever have a day off?" I asked him.

"No, I don't," he replied matter-of-factly.

Another employee worked full-time in a school and added shifts at Walmart. This combination of jobs resulted in very long days of work. A third employee worked in a medical office and added shifts at Walmart. These employees were doing what they had to do to cover their bills. I had no days off when I worked at Lord & Taylor and Italio restaurant. I know what it means to work seven days a week. Probably only someone who has been working multiple jobs can comprehend the sacrifice involved. However, once you get into a work routine, you manage because work becomes part of your daily life. There is no such thing as a vacation, but who needs to go on vacation when you need to raise children, guarantee housing, pay bills, and purchase food. Vacations become a ridiculous luxury. What about college degrees? They provide personal enrichment, but when you need a paycheck fast, they become a luxury as well.

A quick online search produced very few realistic options. I ended up with two job interviews: one for a food delivery position with a pizza company and one for a cashier position with Walmart. Walmart hired me on the spot. Therefore, I never went to my pizza delivery interview. I was hired in June 2022 as a part-time cashier with a pay of $12/hour for about 32 hours a week. Within a few weeks, my pay was raised to $14/hour, as all cashier jobs now started at that rate. Although I was primarily a cashier at one of the registers, occasionally I was sent to monitor the self-scan area. I wasn't trained to work at the customer service desk. Some cashiers are trained to do all three jobs and switch from one to the other as needed. However, the customer service desk doesn't offer a higher pay. It only gives more responsibilities.

My new job had some advantages. I no longer had to drive one hour to reach my place of employment. It was much less complicated than my previous job. It paid me exactly for the hours of work I put in. It ended when I clocked out. Being a part-time worker meant that my hours could decrease during slow times of the year, although they could also increase during busy holiday times. After 20 years in retail, I believe that one should take a job for what it's worth. If it fulfills basic needs, it's acceptable.

Working for a neighborhood grocery store meant that I dealt with the reality of human everyday life. Week after week, customers came into the store to buy milk, eggs, bread, meat, vegetables, and medicines, not luxury items. They bought provisions for themselves and for their family, often with difficulty and with government assistance. We recognized our regular shoppers, although we rarely learned their names. They told us about their ailments, their family members, their pets, their house damages after a hurricane, their food preferences, their social gatherings, their jobs. A neighborhood grocery store is very much like a family environment where everyone speaks a simple language that anyone can understand.

About a year after I was hired, Walmart stopped selling tobacco and cigarettes in our store. This company choice was a healthy one that made me feel good after working as a cashier at Walgreens. Walgreens required that we used a scripted phrase ending with *Be Well*. Customers never responded positively to this unnatural expression.

"Why do you tell people to be well if you sell cigarettes?" one customer said tartly.

Having been a non-smoker all my life, I could see his point although my role in the store didn't allow me to tell him. For years, his comment haunted me and made me feel very guilty for having sold something that can hurt people. I was happy when Walmart didn't place me at the customer service desk because I didn't want to sell cigarettes. When Walmart discontinued the sale of tobacco, it was like ending a bad chapter of my work life.

In my second year of employment, our store underwent a total renovation. The company added self-scan machines and improved the self-scan stations, allowing customers to be very comfortable when making their purchases in that area. The number of cashier-operated registers remained the same. The company seemed to encourage a future of self-scanning, as it decided not to invest in a higher number of regular registers. Although we still provided free plastic bags in Florida, reusable bags were now sold at the registers, suggesting another possible future change.

After the renovation, the employees fulfilling online orders had their enclosed space. Online grocery shopping isn't an alien concept. Many of us like to pick our produce and meats, but there are people who don't have time to shop for groceries in person. Elderly people are very challenged when it comes to buying groceries. They aren't very mobile and can't drive, sometimes.

Many people shop for themselves and also for their elderly mother or father or neighbor or for a sick relative. Then, there are Walmart Spark drivers who shop and deliver groceries to customers. It's impossible to predict at this time if brick-and-mortar grocery stores will become online food fulfillment centers only. It depends on economic changes and on the lifestyle that people will embrace.

There are still many customers who don't like self-scan machines and prefer standing in line at the register to get full service. They say that they are uncomfortable using these machines. They perceive self-scanning and bagging as work that they shouldn't be doing, since there are people already paid to do it. They also feel that they deserve full service because of the high prices in the post-Covid age. At the register, almost all customers complained about prices and blamed the government. Getting full service seemed like an earned gift to them.

One of the primary advantages of ecommerce is the time factor. Customers don't have to drive to a mall, spend time walking to reach a specific store, and then spend more time finding the items to be purchased. Shopping in a mall used to be a social activity. Family members or friends used to spend a day at the mall, have lunch there, and take care of their purchases. Nordstrom used to provide a pianist who entertained the shoppers. Restaurants offered a wide selection of interesting foods at a reasonable price. Life has evolved. Prices have changed. The merchandise selection inside the stores isn't as good as it used to be. Shopping in the mall has become inconvenient. Customer behavior adjusted to a new type of life that includes constant use of AI technology. Major companies keep closing stores nationwide. Online stores are undoubtedly offering competitive discounts and growing. Amazon is probably one of the most successful platforms for online shopping because it offers excellent services. Shipping is very fast and free for Prime members. Returns are very fast. Prices are competitive. Merchandise selection is excellent. Quality is good. Amazon Fresh is the Amazon grocery store, which offers a wide variety of products and competitive low prices. It's a recent concept that includes the online store and physical stores.

Online grocery shopping is an important innovation that will change how we shop and will reshape the way physical stores operate. As companies expand their service capability and technologically integrate and globalize their business branches, they will continue to grow and modify grocery shopping behavior. Sophisticated tools that optimize all phases of company operation, from warehouse automation to delivery drones and virtual carts or smart carts that bypass checkout stations, lead to a future in which online and physical shopping are integrated. The role of cashiers will become completely redundant.

Although we all shop online on a variety of websites, sometimes we discover that some companies take up to three weeks to ship an item, some of them claim that they delivered an item that hasn't been delivered, and some ship damaged merchandise. In 2004, my daughter ordered a bridesmaid dress for my son's wedding, from a website called Ever-Pretty. She received a dress that had a large stain on the chest, numerous holes in the fabric, and pulled threads in the back. The tag was still attached, which suggests that the dress may have been worn by a previous buyer who hid the tag and returned the dress. Ever-Pretty sent my daughter a damaged dress that hadn't been inspected. The company did refund the damaged dress that my daughter sent back. However, the company gained a horrific online review with pictures.

Customers read online reviews, which can be very damaging to a business that cannot fulfill orders properly and ethically. During my training at Macy's, I learned that customer service was essential because each unhappy customer reported his/her bad experience to 12 other people, according to the statistics of that time. Today, social media can empower or damage a company much faster and on a much larger scale. Customers share their experiences with other shoppers. Everyone checks reviews online prior to making an important purchase.

Having been in retail for so many years, I feel compelled to always write a good or bad review when I receive outstanding or terrible service. All shoppers have the responsibility to inform other potential buyers, particularly after a disastrous experience. Online reviews are probably one of the best services offered to all of us by the online markets. Good reviews are legitimately earned with excellent service and quality. Bad reviews are rightfully earned by disregarding the buyers who are actually providing bread and butter to the online sellers. I never forgive a business that betrays me financially because when I offer my money to a company, meaning the money that I earned standing in a store during long shifts, I expect that company to deliver ethically.

They say that all businesses have a life that starts, evolves, and always comes to an end. Some last longer than others. Who would have thought that Blockbuster, a company that made hundreds of small movie rental stores go out of business, would have encountered its own demise? Yet, as we can stream movies on smart TVs now, the movie rental concept has become obsolete.

When a store can't fulfill online orders successfully, it shortens its own lifespan. In September 2024, I placed an online order with my American Express card for a one-pound box of custom chocolates for my daughter's upcoming birthday. Normally, I would have ordered the chocolates on Amazon, but I wanted my daughter to pick the chocolates she liked. Only the See's Candies website allows custom orders. It was a very simple order that appeared to have gone through. A few days later, See's Candies charged and then refunded one dollar on my American Express to check my card. Since I didn't receive an email with a confirmation number and a tracking number, I called the See's customer service.

During my first phone call, the representative found me in the computer system with an incorrect address. She updated my address. She didn't have my phone number and she didn't have my American Express card showing anywhere, although that was the card I used to place my order. She said that she had no order for me. She told me that my chocolates were probably still in the bag and that my order hadn't been processed. She recommended checking my cart and placing the order. I checked the cart, but there was nothing in it. I called back the See's Candies customer service number. The second representative I spoke with confirmed that I had no order. I asked why they had checked my credit card if they had no order.

"See's Candies didn't check your card. Your bank checked your card to see how much money you have in your bank account," was her answer.

"I used an American Express card. Banks don't check bank accounts for credit card orders online," I retorted.

In my mind, I was processing the fact that this customer service representative was talking about the money in my bank account. Her words were inappropriate and devoid of any customer service. I quickly ended my conversation. An American Express phone representative confirmed that See's Candies had checked my card. I decided to block the credit card I had used to place my order and replace it with a new one. Finally, I wrote a terrible online review.

At a time when everyone is challenged by very high prices and chocolates are a commodity that one can live without, See's Candies hadn't fulfilled a simple order, paid with a perfectly good American Express card that had passed its check. My daughter never received her chocolates for her birthday. The See's Candies company mailed me a gift card that I sent back. Will I order chocolates from See's Candies in the future? Probably not, unless I use a loadable card, but definitely never again with a personal credit card because the company lost my trust. Trust is what really matters in a business relationship.

Although the Walmart Neighborhood Market where I worked catered primarily to neighborhood residents, we also had customers who lived in other areas and drove specifically to reach our neighborhood store. They used to say that they preferred the smaller store, which usually has a wider food selection than the large Walmart Supercenter. Some long-time cashiers also seemed to attract the shoppers. One of my coworkers had customers lined up at her register specifically to have a chat with her while she took care of their purchase. Some older customers don't interact with many people during the day. Going to the grocery store is a social event for them.

Most of our customers were recurrent shoppers. They knew where everything was in the store. They knew the cost of their regular products and immediately noticed if any price changed. Like most shoppers nationwide, they went to multiple grocery stores, comparing deals, prices, and quality. In-store grocery shoppers are very sophisticated shoppers. Although they have a favorite store in which they shop, they won't ignore other stores with competitive deals. Even Walmart employees shop in multiple stores. Most of them shop in the Walmart closer to their residence, not the store in which they work. That's convenient. They also shop at a variety of other stores, such as Aldi, Publix, Winn Dixie and so forth. Everyone is after specific products that one store is unable to satisfy completely and deals that are very competitive in different locations. Walmart shoppers are very loyal shoppers who may purchase a few products elsewhere, but they will always come back to Walmart because they are comfortable in their neighborhood store and because they believe that Walmart has the best prices overall. Comfort and trust are fundamental. Grocery shopping, like all shopping, involves a psychological component. Entering the store, a customer recognizes a comfortable and familiar environment. Then, choosing food products is an emotional activity like all types of shopping.

We had affluent shoppers and low-income shoppers. They were all budget-conscious and they all believed that they could save at Walmart. Many customers used a variety of food stamps and health plan benefits. Some of them expected to have their entire grocery purchase covered by food stamps and if there was a remaining balance to be paid, they took food out of their shopping cart at the register.

Some customers asked for two transactions: one to be covered by food stamps, and a separate one for alcohol to be covered with cash. Yet, there were desperate customers seriously trying to survive. On one occasion, a middle-aged man couldn't cover his food purchase entirely with food stamps. After I told him that he still had a remaining amount to pay, he stalled for a while, and finally opened up.

"I live in a car. I don't have any other money," he said.

While I tried to find a manager to help feed this poor man, one of the other cashiers paid with money she had in her pocket. Sometimes, a manager used a personal credit card to cover the remaining part of a purchase that the shopper couldn't pay.

Everyone complained about prices and price increases. No one was satisfied. Customers often reminisced about the past, when the products in their cart used to cost much less. They kept checking the total price, as I was scanning their items. They did everything they could to lower the price, purchasing products on sale or using manufacturers' coupons. They complained about having picked too many products. They waited to see if the final price matched the price they had in mind and, if it didn't, they took products out of their transaction. They expressed their intention of not shopping for at least the next two weeks, which was their way of comforting themselves for the price they had to pay. They explained that they had been tempted by products that weren't in their list. They usually turned down any addition that their child wanted to purchase:

"No, we are not getting this," "No, we can't get this," "No, put it away!" "No, I'm not paying for that," and so forth.

They all seemed to leave financially dissatisfied. Cards didn't always go through, gift cards were empty, food stamps weren't sufficient. Customers juggled themselves between foods they would have liked to eat and the reality of their budget. You need a thick skin to be a cashier in a grocery store at the present time.

Our customers did show community support. When a customer was unable to pay in full and started taking food out of the transaction, often the next customer in line offered to pay the remaining balance. People helped each other. Sadly, some customers took advantage of this generosity. When they had a remaining balance after applying their food stamps, they pretended to be unable to pay for it, stalling the line. If no one offered to cover their balance, they magically pulled cash out of their wallet. There were also very ungrateful customers. One woman, whose food stamps didn't cover her purchase in full, slowed down the line while texting. The next customer offered to pay. She quickly started moving away with her cart, without even thanking the generous customer.

"Just a minute!" I stopped her. "You don't have a receipt and she doesn't have a receipt yet." She stopped and continued texting. As soon as the next customer paid for her bill, she left very quickly without thanking anyone. She seemed to have planned it. Another customer was missing less than a dollar to pay for her purchase in full. I told her that she still had a balance to be paid.

"Do I really have to pay that small amount?" she asked me.

"I can't close the transaction on the register if there is a remaining amount," I told her.

"What do you mean? I do it all the time!" she said, looking at me as if I was crazy. A cashier must have paid for her previously. Now, she expected it. Our managers didn't allow the cashier signed into the register to pay for the purchase. Any other manager or cashier not signed into the register could produce a credit card or cash to complete the transaction. However, the managers started discouraging this practice.

Walmart likes to keep its grocery prices affordable to attract buyers. Customers still shop in multiple stores and seek the lowest price. This happens also in other sectors. Rather than being loyal to a specific brand, customers research and compare prices online, even when they are inside the store. Many companies introduced the "buy online and pick up in store" solution, which is a hybrid form of ecommerce. Self-checkout is gradually becoming more sophisticated through the use of AI. Smart carts are undergoing experimentation. The future of retail workers is gradually changing and narrowing. As robots continue taking over many human responsibilities, fewer employees are needed. Currently, with "Scan-and-go," Walmart customers scan each item they place in their cart using an app on their phone. Then, they pay through the app reducing shopping time. Digital signage capable of updating automatically and smart shelves capable of advertising products and flagging an order when products are sold out can cut stocking time. Electronic advertisement through a store app, such as Publix listing its weekly discounts and BOGO deals, encourages sales. Replacing retail workers with machines may speed up transactions. However, employees using a variety of technological tools may coexist with robots because people do like buying from real people. This may be the only way in which brick-and-mortar stores can continue to remain open.

Our store seemed to have constant cashier coverage problems. They had high turnover. During the three years I worked at Walmart, two cashiers died and one retired. Some cashiers constantly called out sick. Many cashiers quit, some giving proper notice and some disappearing without notice. A few cashiers transferred to Walmart stores in other cities. The managers kept hiring and training new employees. Walmart paid well its cashiers. Some cashiers came to work in our store because their pay per hour in other companies, such as Marshall's, was lower. Yet, there never seemed to be sufficient coverage of the registers or the self-scan area. The managers started closing one of the self-scan lanes for part of the day, when cashiers were particularly low in number.

In 2025, the managers offered a full-time position to me and to another cashier who had been hired a couple of months after me. We were both very reliable. I had never missed one day of work in three years and I showed up on time. The store needed to guarantee steady coverage, which can only be done with full-time cashiers. As the operational manager explained, part-time cashiers were fillers whose schedules were tailored to satisfy the store needs. Instead, a full-time cashier guaranteed 40 hours a week of continuous coverage with an identical schedule every week. I accepted the full-time offer, which was an honor, as it showed the managers' appreciation of my good work and reliability. My pay per hour remained the same, but the extra hours of work each week increased my paycheck significantly. I was earning $14.86/hour, which included two annual raises since my hiring date. I was really happy with my higher paychecks. Additionally, I had a set schedule with two specific days off each week. Unfortunately, a disastrous event impacted my retail work life again. At Lord & Taylor I had fractured my knee and at Neiman Marcus I had developed an unbearable allergic reaction inside the store. At Walmart a new problem surfaced just when I was receiving good paychecks in a logistically ideal situation. I was never meant to be lucky and to enjoy the results of my hard work and reliability.

As I scanned for hours lifting heavy objects, moving them, and bagging them, I gradually developed a mild pain in my right bicep. I started using my right arm less and less, relying on my left arm, but the pain continued to increase and spread along my arm, from my shoulder to my fingers. I usually woke up in the middle of the night and in the morning with excruciating pain. I couldn't move my right arm in many directions, I couldn't raise it, and I couldn't carry anything even mildly heavy without pain. On my days off, I exposed my arm to the hot summer sun, which made me feel better. A little breaststroke in the pool also calmed my pain temporarily.

The earliest medical appointment I was able to set was scheduled four weeks later. As I realized I could no longer continue working on the register, I asked the store managers to allow me to move to the self-scan area. I purchased a phone lanyard that allowed me to carry the store monitoring phone around my neck. It wasn't enough. The cold temperature of the store also magnified my pain. Standing for eight hours in a cold environment with constant pain was draining. My job was no longer sustainable at Walmart. I was unable to move a watermelon that a customer no longer wanted. Having to call a coworker to move a watermelon clearly indicated that I couldn't continue to work in a grocery store. My daughter rightly suggested that eventually, when my arm healed, going back to work on the register and lifting weights while scanning could have caused a relapse in the future. While I was still waiting for the day of my medical appointment, I resigned turning in a two weeks' notice.

My doctor's visit seemed to indicate that my retail work life was over. I had a pinched nerve, caused by a degeneration of my cervical disc, and an inflammation of my tendon and bicep. Degeneration of the cervical disc, which is part of aging, can also be precipitated by prolonged standing with incorrect posture. Twenty years of standing in the stores was catching up with me. I often had a headache and neck pain after my long shifts. I woke up with severe neckache and headache sometimes, but I disregarded them because I had to go to work. My situation was worse than when I resigned from Neiman Marcus. Now, I was unable to work in any retail store. What would have happened if I had been a forty-year-old woman with two children under my care? I was lucky that my children no longer depended on me. Retail is a life saver for many people, particularly single women with children, who have no other way to make a living.

Today, many retail workers barely manage living paycheck to paycheck and frequently change jobs or add multiple jobs trying to keep up with the cost of living. Did they fail the system or is the system failing them? Retail workers are very resilient people who adjust constantly to the system and manage to pay their bills, raise children, purchase necessities, and live with a very low income. Business is not charity. Stores don't cater to the workers. They engage them to fulfill their needs and easily replace them when necessary. Their expectation is: get the job done and if you don't like the pay or anything else, the door is open. There will always be another applicant ready to take that job. Retail workers are constrained in a form of voluntary servitude. The system is never going to provide more money, better hours, and better conditions unless retail workers evolve into irreplaceable, highly trained individuals that use sophisticated sales tools. They will have to change their role and evolve to meet the complex challenges of future retail, addressing in-store and online business in concert.

Only then, as they become essential pawns for a money-making business, their wages may rise.

My personal experience over a period of 20 years is a simple testimonial exemplifying how retail workers struggle to earn a living. Retail work is very hard work, physically and mentally, with a limited compensation. Some people believe that women tend to enter the retail workforce when they get bored at home. I did encounter a widow who chose to work as a cashier at Walmart "to get out of the house." Within a month, she resigned because, as she said, the job was too hard. Retail employment isn't a country club that one joins to socialize. Retail workers stand for hours at a time, day after day, performing tasks to be able to collect a small paycheck. They may have to lift and carry heavy weights regularly, even if they are salespersons. When they are challenged by economic problems stemming from external events, such as the 2008 recession or the Covid outbreak, their work becomes even more arduous.

My heart cries when I see a customer casually insulting an employee who is devoting time and skills to satisfy that customer's needs. A whole life and sometimes an entire family is at stake behind a simple hourly job. Walmart is the only place of work where I witnessed customers making callous comments and yelling at employees. Generally, most of our customers are truly gracious and polite. A restaurant owner, who was paying for his groceries at my register, complimented our store.

"I appreciate what all of you do here. I know how hard your job is," he said.

However, once in a while, a customer verbally attacked an employee who was following procedures to monitor the self-scan area or was asking to check ID in order to release alcohol. A man traveling in his wheelchair liked to give orders and raise his voice while a cashier was helping him. A cashier was very distraught after he left the store one day.

"I really can't take it when they yell at me," she said. Her skin wasn't thick enough for the job yet. In reality, all customers who mistreat employees have a serious personal problem. They take advantage of the employee's vulnerable position. Seasoned employees usually don't react and don't get upset because an insulting customer is irrelevant within the much larger picture of a life with difficulties. Customers who tend to be uncooperative and argumentative in the self-scan area are often not in good faith.

"If he got mad because you took his empty basket, he was probably trying to hide something behind it!" was a typical perceptive comment made by Stacy, who had been working in the self-scan area for many years. Stacy was friendly with all customers, knew all the regular ones, ignored men calling her "Sweetie," and always caught the customer who was about to carry out a prohibited step. She wasn't really someone I would call "Sweetie." Behind her outgoing attitude, there was a tough employee, with an icy stare, who rarely smiled and never missed anything. She protected the self-scan area very efficiently.

When I was hired at Linens 'n Things, Linda, the Bedding manager, was concerned about the fact that I was very inexperienced and unprepared to deal with a possible customer treating me roughly.

"If anyone is ever disrespectful to you, let me know. I will take care of it," she told me.

No one ever disrespected me at Linens 'n Things nor in the stores that followed, until I reached Walmart, the only store where one customer overstepped his boundaries. While I was scanning his items, he unleashed a very rude comment.

"Are you an expensive date?" he asked me. Had I been in my 20s, 30s, or 40s, I would have been just as astonished as I was now, in my 70s.

"What?" was my reaction.

"You heard me right!" he continued. "Are you an expensive date?" he repeated, as if I was some kind of merchandise to be purchased.

The cool-headed composure I acquired living with an abusive husband and working in retail for many years guided me.

"I have no price," was my flat answer.

Clearly, a man who verbally violates a female cashier, regardless of age, because she's in a vulnerable position, has serious personal problems dealing with women. That didn't give him the right to be disrespectful. I wasn't happy with my reaction, which was limited by the nature of my job, as I'm required to remain controlled with the public. Yet, I really wasn't satisfied with my answer because this shameful man had not only insulted me, but also the working category of women cashiers and the company that I was representing in my cashier role. Months later, he reappeared in front of my register.

"You're an expensive date," he blurted out offensively, trying to provoke my reaction again. It was humiliating. He needed a firm answer that could shield me, other women cashiers, and my company.

"I'm not a date. I am an honest woman who works at Walmart as a cashier," I said looking straight in his face.

He seemed crestfallen, although he didn't understand the reality of the retail world, which he was disrespecting so casually. I was happy I had put him in his place decisively and within the verbal limitations of my employment position. The women in line after him addressed me in a very cordial manner. They understood.

My heart also cries when a manager unjustly disregards or disrespects an employee. Being in a leadership position is a high responsibility that goes beyond a paycheck. The two managers who fired me at Sears during my training period didn't know that I had just gone through two knee surgeries, months of physical rehabilitation, and a city relocation. Regardless of whether their decision had been financially motivated by a struggling store or by the fact that they truly didn't like me, these two managers had used their leadership position to throw a working woman into unemployment, for no legitimate reason. They should have never been empowered to manage human resources. Everyone counts. I'm not surprised that the store shut down soon afterwards.

I hope that my story will shed some light on the difficult role that workers assume in retail. They deserve recognition because in many ways they are heroes within our social structure. They accept a job with low hourly pay to solve existential problems. They frantically change job after job trying to find an acceptable situation. They lose their job due to reasons outside of their control. They take more than one job at a time seeking financial improvement. They organize their life and their family life around their schedules, always abiding by the rules and following procedures. That's how millions of people live. I hope that my book gives them a voice, while they are working and struggling, unrecognized in the dark. My twenty years of retail work will have served a higher purpose then.